Nurturing Strangeı

MW01046704

Nurturing Strangers focuses on loving nonviolent re-parenting of children in foster care. This book is a jargon-free mix of narrative and real-life case studies, together with the theory and practice of nonviolence. *Nurturing Strangers* and the authors' previous book, *Welcoming Strangers*, are the first books to apply philosophies of nonviolence directly to the care of children in the foster care system. One of the many strengths of these books are that they are not merely theoretical, but rooted in the practice of nonviolence incorporated into work with children for over thirty years. *Nurturing Strangers* is for foster carers, caseworkers, case managers, social work students, and parents, as well as the general reader interested in children who have been victims of violence in and out of the foster care system.

Andrew Fitz-Gibbon, a Fellow of the Royal Society of Arts, is Professor of Philosophy, Chair of the Philosophy Department, and Director of the Center for Ethics, Peace and Social Justice, at the State University of New York College at Cortland. He is the author, co-author or editor of thirteen books.

Jane Hall Fitz-Gibbon works in crisis support with TST BOCES, and is involved with the Department of Social Services, co-leading courses on foster care, adoption, and child sexual abuse. Her latest book, *Corporal Punishment, Religion and United States Public Schools*, was published by Palgrave Macmillan in 2017.

This gem of a book is an insightful guide for all caregivers who want to be a positive influence in the lives of children. The authors share touching stories and practical advice from their lives as foster parents. Their enlightened approach is a beautiful testament of the power of positive parenting.
—**Tina McMechen**, Acting Director, and Genevieve Rivera, Managing Director, American Society for the Positive Care of Children

Rather than simply being a list of "shoulds" and "shouldn'ts", this book provides perspectives on the topic of "re-parenting" children who have experienced significant trauma and chaos. This book is not just an academic treatise. Its strength lies with its real-world view of working with these kids. Readers will walk away with a different perspective of the children they care for, and of themselves as caregivers. They will gain useful ideas for dealing with difficult situations, and they will gain an understanding that even when you do *everything* right, things may not always work out the way they would like. Knowing that might just help the exhausted, frustrated foster parent to provide the most nurturing environment possible.
—**Raymond D. Collings**, Associate Professor, Psychology, State University of New York, Cortland

Nurturing Strangers

Strategies for Nonviolent Re-parenting of Children in Foster Care

Andrew Fitz-Gibbon and Jane Hall Fitz-Gibbon

Routledge
Taylor & Francis Group

NEW YORK AND LONDON

First published 2019
by Routledge
52 Vanderbilt Avenue, New York, NY 10017

and by Routledge
2 Park Square, Milton Park, Abingdon, Oxon, OX14 4RN

Routledge is an imprint of the Taylor & Francis Group, an informa business

Library of Congress Cataloging-in-Publication Data
A catalog record for this title has been requested

ISBN: 978-1-138-50316-8 (hbk)
ISBN: 978-1-138-50317-5 (pbk)
ISBN: 978-1-315-14525-9 (ebk)

Typeset in Bembo
by Swales & Willis Ltd, Exeter, Devon, UK

To our siblings
Sandra, Jenny, Spencer,
Jackie and Debbie

Contents

Acknowledgments

Welcoming Strangers, published in 2016, was intended to be the swansong to our foster care career. We had enjoyed the ride, hopefully done good in our small world, and had something to pass on to others—the practice we had begun to term "loving nonviolent re-parenting." The publication of the book, our sixth written together, was to mark our retirement from actively caring for children, though Jane had intended to keep in contact with our local foster carers and adopters through the support group she organizes. However, circumstances dictated otherwise. Not long after the publication of *Welcoming Strangers*, Kristen Monroe, Commissioner for Social Services of Cortland County, NY—who kindly wrote the foreword to this book—asked if we could conduct training for foster parents and caseworkers in nonviolent care. We readily agreed. Three courses, and a few more children later, with interest from another fourteen counties and agencies in New York, our involvement in foster care has taken a turn toward training others in loving nonviolent re-parenting.

Welcoming Strangers was part narrative—telling the journey of our work with children in care—and part the application of the principles of loving nonviolence to the daunting task of helping children to heal from trauma caused by violence. We continue the format of story-telling and the application of principles in *Nurturing Strangers*. In *Welcoming Strangers*, we introduced the term "re-parent" to indicate that children in foster care have been parented already, often in inadequate ways. Our observation is that all children in care are victims of violence in one or several ways—physical, sexual, emotional, and systemic, and that this violence traumatizes children in different ways. Some seem to weather the storm better than others, but for most the effects of trauma can be seen in related behavior—withdrawal, violence, stealing, and eating disorders, to name only a few—and in difficult relationships. Deprived of love, safety, and adequate nurturance in their birth homes, and exhibiting behavior readily thought of as "naughty," with the associated label "bad kid," children in foster care present a challenge to even the most experienced re-parents. Our approach to help children recover from trauma induced by violence has been to create a loving environment where intentional nonviolence is practied. Nonviolence is a way of living that seeks to reduce violence:

- by refraining from violent actions;
- by acting according to loving kindness; and
- by seeking the good for the Other.

Though simple in the saying, intentional nonviolence requires a great deal of work on the part of the carers. Most of us, even those who have not been victims of violence, have internalized the view that violence works as a last resort—the myth of redemptive violence—and that this strategy will work with children too. Here we present a different approach rooted in our experience of caring for over thirty years, and based on good philosophical reasoning.

In writing *Nurturing Strangers* we would like to thank Kristen Monroe, Commissioner of Social Services, Allison Veintimilla, Director of Social Services, and their staff in Cortland County, NY, for the courage to adopt loving nonviolence in training carers and caseworkers; the advisory board of the Welcoming Strangers Project at SUNY Cortland; Tom Frank, and Liz Speziale from Research and Sponsored Programs; Leslie Eaton for analysis of the data from our courses; and Michael Emmart and Pam Talbott for help and support; Karla Alwes provided impeccable editing, and Craig Hanson gave us helpful comments on addiction.

All the stories we tell are true, though we have changed names, genders, and details for the sake of anonymity.

Jane Hall Fitz-Gibbon
Andrew Fitz-Gibbon
SUNY Cortland, Summer 2018

Foreword

Be prepared for Jane and Andy Fitz-Gibbon to take you on a thought-provoking journey as you consider your private emotional responses, biases, values, and moral strengths. The ideas and experiences shared in *Nurturing Strangers* will leave you pondering the ways in which you respond to others, and whether those responses make you proudest. I wish I had been able to take that journey 27 years ago when I was hired as a foster care caseworker in a rural upstate New York county.

Like many of my peers at the time, I was fresh out of college, with no understanding of the social services system or its purpose, having had the good fortune of being raised by very nurturing, loving parents. With a mother who taught first grade and a father who ran a small business, my needs were fully met. I had never heard about Child Protective Services. I look back on my two years as a caseworker and feel an inadequacy for the work. Sure, I was an ace at making my contacts, doing paperwork and completing all required case transactions, but I now realize how ineffective I was at advocating for traumatized children and supporting their caretakers when faced with unimaginable behaviors. Although I had studied early childhood development and could identify delays in children, I had never learned about the significant role trauma played in those delays, and I certainly had never learned strategies to help caretakers positively address challenging behaviors.

Jane and Andy bring to life and fully articulate a notion that was just beginning to surface in my early experiences. That is, if severely traumatized children are removed from an environment full of violence that lacks essential nurturing and are put into one that provides a loving non-violent commitment and structure with consistency, empathy, and trustworthy adults who see to their safety and well-being, children will begin to heal. In this book, they continue to build upon their nonviolent re-parenting ideas shared in *Welcoming Strangers* using a framework provided by psychologist Steven Pinker and the social building blocks of empathy, self-control, moral sense and reason. Readers will be inspired and perhaps question if they would have the strength needed to help our most vulnerable children.

Anyone who cares for traumatized children, or in some way influences the decisions that affect them, will be stronger for reading this book. As an administrator in that same rural county, I am responsible for establishing policies regarding out of home placements of children. Our system and partners in the juvenile justice system, schools, and treatment arena have come a long way since I was a young caseworker in understanding the effects of trauma on children. Although the system has primarily swung away from the use of placements in detention and residential care as punishment for ill-behaved children, we can all do more to challenge our conventional thinking and to address the new challenges created by an increased use of family foster care.

I first met Andy by chance at a meeting with another local college professor to exchange perspectives about our social services foster care system. It was there I learned about the first book he and Jane were publishing about nonviolent re-parenting. I was intrigued because their ideas address some of the biggest struggles we face in our family foster care program.

We recruit wonderful people to be foster parents, but have lost far too many due to the complex needs of traumatized children. Some only have their experiences with healthy untraumatized children on which to base their expectations and disappointments. Jane and Andy's writings have helped identify behaviors, skills and knowledge that affect the varying levels of tolerance for challenging behaviors we see in our family foster care homes. Some well-intended parents refuse future placements after one bad event while others continue welcoming new placements no matter how many times their cars are stolen, walls need repair, or hearts are broken. I knew they could help us improve our understanding of what foster parents experience and how to better support them.

Jane and Andy developed and provided a ten-week training course for our foster parents and casework staff. The feedback was tremendous. For the first time, we were offering a training by people who have over 30 years of experience living through the good and bad that comes with re-parenting. They helped our foster parents, who so desperately want to nurture our most vulnerable children, recognize how everything they do and say as caretakers has an impact. Their use of real stories, practical strategies, and explanations of psychological and philosophical considerations engage their audience to internalize these concepts in powerful ways.

The impact of this book cannot be over-stated. The more I read their work, the more I understand and feel empowered to make real changes in the work we do for children and their families. This book gives strength to those who are bravely re-parenting children by recognizing that such work is never fully mastered, but is always enhanced by those who allow themselves the ability to learn from every experience.

I cannot help but frame the importance of the book around my own experiences. Although I encountered very little violence and a childhood filled with loving family memories, I still remember the few times I experienced a (then acceptable) spanking. It is remarkable given a childhood predominately filled with loving family experiences that I even remember those isolated minor traumatic events. How difficult it is to contemplate the pain that must be harbored by a child exposed to in-home violence day after day.

Nurturing Strangers will provide readers with hope and a genuine feeling for the joys and sorrows experienced when helping traumatized children heal. Readers will be engaged to consider their own roles in the lives of children and how they too might apply the ideas to ensure they are seizing all opportunities to role-model empathy, self-control, reasoning and non-violence while affirming the self-worth of children. I am left hoping Jane and Andy continue to share their thoughts about the essential work of re-parenting and consider how their work might be extended to the entire system of care givers for our most vulnerable children.

The views and thoughts expressed above are solely my own and do not necessarily represent those of the Department of Social Services.

Kristen Monroe
Commissioner, Department of Social Services, Cortland County, NY

1 Re-visiting Loving Nonviolent Re-parenting

In *Welcoming Strangers*, we told our story of how for over 34 years we opened our home to children who, for one reason or another, could not live with their birth families. Most of these children suffered trauma related to violence in its many forms—physical, psychological, sexual, and systemic. Welcoming these young strangers into our home was, for them, only the beginning of a long process toward healing and responsible adulthood. We realized early on that we needed to find ways to provide ongoing nurture that would help our children heal from their difficult start. Trauma takes time to heal, and violence induced trauma takes longer to heal than a few short months, or even several years. Sadly, some struggle with the ravages of abuse or neglect well into their adult lives. Some never completely get over it, and the effect of trauma marks their whole lives. Our loving nonviolent care of children is only a step on the journey toward their well-being. It has been a highlight of our years as foster carers to hear that some of the children we welcomed and nurtured have done well, some now in their thirties with families of their own.

*

"I made the academic dean's list for the third semester in a row," Hannah proudly announced on social media. For Hannah, even to be in college was an amazing feat that had taken lots of perseverance, determination, and courage, as she overcame many obstacles.

*

"I'm back in your town for the weekend. Can I come and see you?" Julianna arrived complete with pastry treats for the family. We spent the afternoon listening to the stories of her many successes and reminiscing about the past.

*

"Will you come to my wedding? There is an invitation in the mail." LeShaun texted us. "I really want you to be there."

*

Xavier's Facebook comment made us smile. In response to a report of a local burglary he wrote sarcastically, "Geez, they need to start robbing job applications." At least, we had instilled a work ethic in him!

*

Placing the baby gingerly in Jane's arms, Shelley said "You're the only people the baby will call grandma and grandad."

*

Jonathon oozed pride as he told us on social media that just as we had taken him, and our other children strawberry picking each June, he now wanted take his own two children. "It was one of my highlights growing up," he said.

*

To parent children is the most natural of activities. Like the other mammals, the human animal throughout its evolution has continued the biological function of the care of the young. We know this is true because to raise successfully an infant to adulthood requires at least a modicum of care. Without care we fail to thrive, and the human animal has been one of the most successful species. Yet, for humans, life appears more complex than for the other mammals. Beside our natural instinct to reproduce and care for our young, our lives are complicated by issues such as values and choices. Our values tell us that some ways of doing things are better than others, and some ways worse than others. For example, we can imagine some ways of caring for the young that are better than others—better for society, better for the child herself, better for the care giver. We would likely say to train a child in good manners through repeated painful electric shocks, or through constant shouting and nagging, is worse than training the child through example and reward. We base our distinctions on our values—we value pleasure over pain, we value kindness over vindictiveness. Having such distinctions based on our values makes sense to us. The human penchant for valuing some things more than others is part and parcel of our meaning-making habit. When we speak of values, of some things being better (more valued) than other things, we enter the tricky world of morality (which we cover more fully in chapter four). We speak of good and bad, of right and wrong, and we make judgments. Human culture is full of value creation, evolution, and sometimes revolution, and that makes natural tasks, such as the care of the young, extraordinarily complex. Values change, and as they do so expectations of that which is socially appropriate, or approved, change with them. In some cultures, as was the case in most western countries until very recently, it was socially acceptable for parents, and teachers *in loco parentis*, to beat a child severely who was wayward or disobedient. Obedience was valued highly, and if in order to make a child obedient the child had to suffer physical pain, then so be it. Our culture valued obedience more highly than it valued freedom from pain for the young. Values change, and today in more and more countries and cultures, physically beating a child is more often than not frowned upon. Even so, in the United States, many still believe that violence works as an effective means of nurturing children. Seventy-six percent of males and 65 percent of females believe that a child needs a "good hard spanking" every now and then. Ninety-four percent of parents with children ages three to four had spanked their children in the course of a year.[1] In other words, most people reserve the "right" to use violence on children when other means have been exhausted. In reality, without internalizing the principles of nonviolence, parents often quickly exhaust "other means," and adults cause pain to children in the mistaken belief that inflicting pain changes behavior. For most of us, our approach to childcare is compounded by the difficulties of dealing with our own inner violence. To differing degrees, all people have the potentiality for violence, and frustrations become anger that in turn becomes rage, resulting often in lashing out verbally, and on too many occasions using physical violence. In caring for children with loving nonviolence, each parent or re-parent, must face their own inner violence and tendency to hurt others.

We are in a cultural space where social practices of parenting are in flux. Parents are often unsure of the social and moral expectations placed upon them. Manuel might come to believe that he ought not to beat his son, but in his youth Manuel's father had beaten him. Manuel internalized the role of "father as tough disciplinarian," but he is conflicted now as social mores are changing.

As a society, too, we have changed perceptions of acceptable child care practice. Not many centuries ago, when all families, more or less, lived in poverty, often all shared a single bedroom—mother, father, seven children, and an unmarried aunt or two. Today, though children can share a bedroom, social services might step in and possibly remove the children as victims of neglect, as ten people in a single bedroom is considered unacceptable. Our understanding of neglect has changed dramatically over the last century, and the whole family sharing a single room would count as neglectful of the children. To be sure, we asked our daughter and daughter-in-law, one a senior caseworker and the other a children's lawyer. They of course confirmed that what was once acceptable is no longer so. Values have changed, and so have expectations. The senior caseworker assured us that everything would be done to keep the family together, but some form of intervention would likely be necessary.

Issues are exacerbated when we consider child abuse. Though what we think of today as child abuse has most likely been the lot of many children in every age, it was not until the 1960s that, as a society, we began to think of certain practices as abusive, harmful to the health of children, and therefore morally wrong. According to the World Health Organization:

> For a long time also there have existed charitable groups and others concerned with children's well-being who have advocated the protection of children. Nevertheless, the issue did not receive widespread attention by the medical profession or the general public until 1962, with the publication of a seminal work, *The Battered Child Syndrome*, by Kempe et al.[2]

Since then, our collective awareness of child neglect has grown exponentially. Though reporting of child abuse has risen, it is likely that we are just becoming aware of what has always been there, and giving to it a different name. Rather than the plight of children getting worse, psychologist Steven Pinker argues that the lot of children in developed countries has never been better. In earlier cultures society accepted:

> The sacrifice of children to gods; the sale of children into slavery, marriage, and religious servitude; the exploitation of children to clean chimneys and crawl through tunnels in coal mines; and the subjection of children to forms of corporal punishment that verge on or cross over into torture.[3]

That we no longer accept, but rather condemn, these practices we regard as progress, and cultural understanding of children and childhood has changed dramatically. Nevertheless, values with regard to children and violence are in a state of flux. Loving nonviolent re-parenting, for which we made the case in *Welcoming Strangers*, and in this book, reflects that cultural shift. Though society has made much progress, more can be done, and children who have suffered the trauma of violence in the home can begin to find healing through loving nonviolent care.

Even though the parental task is a natural one, our ability to make choices means that we are not necessarily bound to do "what comes naturally." People can choose not to breed, and by all accounts many take this path. The data show that the fertility rate (that is, live births per female) dropped worldwide from 5.068 in 1964 to 2.453 in 2015.[4] In many countries the fertility rate has dropped well below the 2.1 births required to keep a population stable by births alone. For example, Greece has a rate of 1.3; Iran 1.7; Korea 1.2; and North America 1.8. Not all people, then, take on the parenting role, but most do at some point in their lives. Beside natural births, people adopt children, care for the offspring of relatives, and look after children on behalf of the state when birth parents can no longer care, or care adequately, for their children. While different cultures conceive the parental roles between women and men differently—and changes happen over time in any culture—the fact that the helpless child of the human animal needs to be tended over a number of years makes parenting as natural an activity as we can imagine.

However, not all parenting is equal. To be a parent of a child requires hard work and the learning of a certain skill set. Some take to the parenting task more easily than others. All make mistakes. Yet, most do a reasonable job and the majority of children grow into socially adept adults, who, more or less, make a decent stab at adulthood. However, those of us who work in foster care see our share of those children who have been parented inadequately, and who carry the trauma of their chaotic and violent upbringing.

If parenting children well is a difficult task, re-parenting children who have experienced violence is frustratingly challenging.

For these reasons, in *Welcoming Strangers* we focused mostly on the kinds of people we need to become in order to provide just such a loving nonviolent environment. To help work this through, we looked at the threefold process of *conscientization* (becoming aware of the violence children have suffered), *internalization* (reflecting on the needs of children and nonviolent strategies to meet those needs), and *intentionalization* (making the choice to become an intentionally nonviolent person). This process involves the psychological triumvirate of feeling, thinking and choosing—feeling, as the re-parent develops empathy for the child; thinking, as she develops strategies for intentional nonviolence; and acting, as he marshals thoughts and feelings in effective nonviolent, practical caring.

We found most help in an ancient strategy sometimes termed "virtue ethics," shared by many in the ancient world in both the West and East. Virtue, an out-of-fashion word that mostly conjures images of Victorian prudery, is often associated with strict rules of sexual propriety. The virtuous person (usually the female), in this caricature, behaves in sexually appropriate ways. This image is unfortunate, for in the ancient world virtue signified the whole character of a person. The virtuous person was one who lived in a way that led toward well-being for themselves and those around them. In other words, a person of virtue lived a good and well-rounded life. In the West, the Greek philosopher Aristotle spoke of a life of *eudaimonia*, well-being, flourishing. Confucius spoke of *ren*, humaneness, as the goal of a virtuous life.

In *Welcoming Strangers*, we took this ancient wisdom and applied it to caring for children who have been traumatized through violence. This approach suggests that to act consistently in loving nonviolent ways, the carer has to become a loving nonviolent person, and becomes such by building small daily habits of loving nonviolence. Of course, no parent or re-parent has the luxury of waiting to care until she becomes such a virtuous person. In Confucian terms, you care for children "as-if" you are already a loving nonviolent person, and over time your character is shaped by your daily habits. We look at this further in chapter four below.

In *Welcoming Strangers*, we suggested that loving nonviolent habits included the following: doing good, not-harming, keeping faith, repairing wrongs and forgiving, treating fairly and equally, respecting with attentiveness, being thankful, caring, being courageous, acting kindly and gently, acting moderately, and not possessing. Our list was not meant to be exhaustive, but rather that intentionally loving nonviolent care looks "something like this." Intentionally choosing to build habits such as these, on a day-to-day, mundane basis, over time produces the virtue of loving nonviolence that we think is essential to care for children who have been victims of violence.

Nurturing Strangers

When we had completed *Welcoming Strangers* we knew we had more to say, but at the time were content to let it be. Since its publication, with our increased role in training others, we realized that we needed to add to what we had said already, hence the present book. Here we consider more carefully some subjects we barely touched on (race and gender issues, for instance), look more closely at issues that people raised with us after reading the first book, and tackle subjects that emerged during the training courses we subsequently developed.

We have subtitled this book, at the suggestion of our editor, "Strategies for Nonviolent Re-parenting of Children in Foster Care." The word "strategy" has a military etymology—in the ancient Greek world, *strategia* is a military term. The general commands the battle, and his skill set was known as generalship. The strategy is the plan of action; the overall design of how to win in a conflict. The military metaphor is an ironic word choice when we want to talk about nonviolence! Even so, it serves its purpose. If we are going to become the loving, nonviolent re-parents of violently traumatized children, what's the plan? What does the overall map look like? A strategy is not the minute details, but rather the bigger picture. In other words, by strategy we don't mean the nuts and bolts of day to day care (though we will cover these in the stories we tell). We mean, rather, the overarching goal toward which we need to move. We will not look so much at "what to do when my two-year-old is screaming before bed and throwing things around the room." Books aplenty have been published in this area. We are more interested in helping carers become the kinds of loving nonviolent people who will be able to work with any traumatized child in any circumstance. Our argument in *Welcoming Strangers* was that care givers who internalize the principles of loving nonviolence will be better prepared to care for children who have experienced the trauma of violence. In other words, we focused mostly on the carer, and not the child in their care. Similarly, in this book we focus on a strategy for becoming a nonviolent re-parent, with the understanding that an intentional commitment and practice of nonviolence, and creating a loving nonviolent home, will help most children in our care begin to experience healing from their traumatic past.

We are aware that our approach—re-parenting in homes committed to loving nonviolence—is just one facet of a many-layered approach that is required to care for traumatized children, and we are not dismissive of the many services provided for children in care. However, by focusing on the carer, we want to redress an imbalance in two ways. First, by taking a "child first" approach, which was itself necessary to correct a "top down" approach to care—and which we broadly agree with—because little has been done to consider the carers themselves. Second, much weight has been placed on professional services for children in care—chiefly counseling services and medication.

Therapy and Pharmacology

Many of the children we have cared for have a mental health diagnosis. Our experience is confirmed by the data for children in foster care:

- 40% born with low birth weight or premature;
- 80% prenatally exposed to substances;
- 30–80% with at least one chronic medical condition [e.g., asthma, HIV, TB];
- 30–50% with dental decay;
- 25% with three or more chronic health problems;
- 30–60% with developmental delays;
- 50–80% with mental and behavioral health problems;
- 20% fully handicapped; and
- 30–40% receiving special education services.[5]

In their journal article, "Mental Health Problems of Children in Foster Care," Clausen et al. carry out a comparative analysis on the subject that includes their own research in three Californian counties. They conclude:

> This multi-site study replicates and extends previous research, conducted in other states which indicate that children in foster care demonstrate very high levels of mental health and behavior problems, as well as significant adaptive functioning deficits. Seventy-five to eighty percent of school age children scored in the problematic range (either clinical or borderline) on one or both of the behavior problem and social competence domains of the CBCL [Child Behavior Checklist].[6]

Many of the children we have cared for in the last fifteen years have made the weekly trip to receive their counseling. Most of our children, too, have been given a mental health diagnosis, often with a variety of medications to treat the condition, accompanied by other medications to treat the side effects of the first set. We have sometimes been bewildered by the multiplicity of drugs prescribed to children in care.

*

Pete sat nervously on the edge of our sofa. We were meeting him for the first time. He was a young man with a great sense of humor, with a winsome and cheeky smile. His background was one of extreme violence exacerbated by family addictions. Pete's story was very sad, causing us to reflect to each other on hearing the tale, "Poor kid, he didn't stand a chance." As he entered his teenage years he had been increasingly out of control at home and at school. Ultimately, he was given a residential placement that lasted nearly two years. In the last few months, against all the odds, he had begun to do well in his placement. Social services wanted to place him in a foster home as a bridge toward his goal of returning to his birth parents; hence, his visit to meet us. A few days later he moved in. Though he brought none with him, he informed us that he took "a shitload of meds." Knowing the dangers in even a few days without long-term medications, we made hasty phone calls, and a few days later the medication arrived by registered mail in a large white paper packet. The ill-fitting package was bursting at the seams, and contained no less than thirteen bottles of pills. After carefully reading the labels, and taking note of dates and prescriptions, and though we found that four of the bottles were out of date, or duplicated, we worked out that Pete was currently taking six different medications on a daily basis, plus an additional three to be given as needed:

Olanzaphine: 10 mg. Two prescriptions: one to take in the morning and one to take in evening. According to our brief research at the time, Olanzaphine is an antipsychotic used to treat schizophrenia and bipolar disorder.

Clonidine: 0.1 mg. One pill at noon, one in the evening. Clonidine is used for a variety of things, but usually ADHD.

Desmopressin: 0.2 mg. One pill in the evening. This is used to treat enuresis.

Methylphenidate: 36 mg. One pill in the morning. Methylphenidate is also called Ritalin, and is used for ADHD.

Divalproex Sodium: 250 mg. One pill in the morning, and two at bedtime. This medication is used as an anticonvulsant, but also to treat manic bipolar disorder.

Famotidine: 40 mg. One pill in the morning. Famotidine is commonly used to treat acid reflux disease.

To be given as needed:

Cetirizine: 10 mg. For allergies.

Promethazine: 25 mg. For nausea and vomiting.

Ventolin. For asthma.

*

One of the most significant books in recent years looking at childhood trauma is psychiatrist Bessel van der Kolk's *The Body Keeps the Score*.[7] Van der Kolk's book is a careful and intriguing account of the developments of psychiatry in helping traumatized people over his 35-year career. Trauma is tantalizingly difficult to understand, let alone resolve, and according to van der Kolk, psychiatrists have broadly tried two approaches: talk therapy and pharmacology. He reports that therapy has been a mixed bag, helping some but not all. He states, "In fact, even reliving the trauma repeatedly in therapy may reinforce preoccupation and fixation."[8] For that, and other reasons, many psychiatrists sought an answer to trauma through drugs, and van der Kolk acknowledges that pharmacology revolutionized the practice of psychiatry. Nonetheless, he comments, "The drug revolution that started out with so much promise may in the end have done as much harm as good . . . In many places drugs have displaced therapy and enabled patients to suppress their problems without addressing underlying issues."[9]

It is standard practice for children in care who display symptoms of trauma to be assessed by psychiatrists. In line with the general trend noted by van der Kolk, children have also been prescribed psychotropic drugs at an alarming rate. He states, "Children from low-income families are four times as likely as privately insured children to receive antipsychotic medicines. These medications often are used to make abused and neglected children more tractable."[10] By all accounts, though drugs can modify behavior, the underlying traumatic condition is left untouched, unless other approaches to care and healing of trauma are utilized.

*

Juanita and Rhianna were unrelated, and placed with us at different times. They had never met each other, but were both thirteen-year-old girls with serious mental health diagnoses: ADHD and bipolar disorder, with the possibility of other significant psychiatric problems. Both were on several different medications. Though their diagnoses were similar, they reacted in completely different ways to the medication.

"I'm not taking my meds this morning," Juanita shouted. This was a regular occurrence at least a couple of times a week. "I hate it. I don't feel like myself when I take it. I'M NOT FUCKING TAKING IT."

As foster carers, we can administer prescribed medication, and encourage children to take their meds. Yet, care givers cannot force medications on an unwilling teen. We would talk to Juanita about how unwise it was not to take the medication, and encourage her to talk to her pediatrician about changing the prescription. Still, on the days she refused to take her meds nothing we could say would make a difference.

Rhianna was just the opposite. She had convinced herself that she couldn't function without the medication. She was terribly anxious about forgetting a dose. We continually reminded her that this was not her responsibility, as Jane administered all meds. Several times we received phone calls from the school, saying that Rhianna couldn't remember if she had taken the medication. Each time she was in tears in the nurse's office. Rhianna was convinced that she couldn't go to class if she hadn't had medication. Each time, Jane gave an assurance to the nurse that Rhianna had taken the medication. On being reassured, Rhianna's day would start to improve. Though given similar diagnoses and medication, the girls faced differing problems. One felt the medications masked her personality, and the other had become so dependent on her meds that she felt she couldn't function without them.

*

For other children, medication was hugely positive. Kevin was a lively eleven-year-old, diagnosed with ADHD. But what a difference his medication made! For the half hour between waking up and the medication starting to work, he was "all over the place." Kevin could not keep his body, or his mind, still. He seemed to bounce around the house talking non-stop. It was difficult to watch him struggle to keep some control of himself. Yet, once in his system, the medication made such a difference to his well-being. Kevin was successful at home and at school, and we were so grateful.

*

Counseling too has produced mixed results. We have had children who have benefitted from it and others where counseling has been not so effective. After a successful year, TJ was leaving us. Although he had experienced multiple traumas in his young life, TJ had responded to loving, nonviolent re-parenting and was doing well at home and at school. However, leaving us meant that another change was looming large in his horizon. TJ was unable to return home due to continued addiction problems in the family, but was given the opportunity to go and live with a close relative who lived in another state over a thousand miles away. In part, TJ was excited at the thought of going, yet he had many concerns. Though his relative had made the long journey to meet him several times, TJ would be leaving our home and friends to go to a largely unknown situation. For TJ the most distressing thought was leaving two little half-sisters. They weren't placed with us, but placed nearby. TJ had spent lots of time with his siblings. The half-sisters were not related to the family with whom TJ was to live, and it would be a hard separation, despite plans for continued contact and visits. The caseworker suggested counseling to help TJ cope with the change. The counseling would be short term (not usually ideal), as the move was to happen in two months coinciding with the end of the school year. Only six counseling appointments were made, yet they helped a great deal. For TJ, the counselor, as a previously unknown person, but with whom he could share all his worries and hopes, was an amazing gift.

*

Counseling was not so helpful for Morgan. While she enjoyed going, and liked her counselor, Morgan refused to talk about any of the various traumas in her life. She found it hard to develop trust, and was very clear that she was never going to talk about "the past" or "her feelings." Ultimately, time may have changed her attitude toward counseling, but it never did in the eighteen months Morgan was with us. She was resolute in refusing help.

*

We do not want to imply that medical and therapeutic approaches are ineffective. We have seen many children helped to function better on a daily basis by their "meds," and others who have worked through difficult issues with competent counselors. However, we do want to raise a note of caution that to rely on such services without placing equal weight on day-to-day care by intentional loving nonviolent re-parents, will not serve the best needs of our children. In our thirty-five years' work in foster care we have never attended training sessions that looked at the kind of people we need to become, nor at the type of home environment that we need to provide, in order to care for children who have been traumatized by violence. Again, this is not to eschew either counseling services for children in care, nor the carefully considered prescription of psychotropic drugs, but it is to say that the daily experience of safety in a nonviolent home, with nonviolent re-parents, plays a vital part in helping children move beyond their trauma.

The Autonomic Nervous System, Violence, Stress and Loving Nonviolence

A factor we barely touched on in *Welcoming Strangers* is the connection between violence, stress and well-being. For many years Andy has taught seminars and workshops in stress management. He designed a for-credit course for undergraduate students to learn how breath meditation and sim-ple *taijiquan* and *qigong* exercises can add to their well-being. Every semester, students report how valuable the class has been in helping them de-stress, especially during exam times. All those who work with today's undergradu-ate population realize how much stress students are under, with referrals to college counseling services continuing to rise. In the class, Andy helps students learn about the autonomic nervous system (ANS). The ANS is a beautifully intricate system in two parts, the sympathetic and the parasym-pathetic. The sympathetic is the "fight, flight, or freeze" response to stressful situations, common to all animals with a developed central nervous system. In females, the sympathetic response to stress is termed tend and befriend, a natural function in response to threat and the care of the young. The parasympathetic—"feed and breed"—is the natural relaxed state, allowing the optimum functions of digestion, reproduction, and a general recharg-ing of the body's systems. Optimally, the system functions in balance for maximum well-being. This sympathetic response is essential for survival. When stressed, the sympathetic response is activated and the parasympa-thetic response suppressed. This is amazingly good to escape from threats, or to protect the young. When switched on through excitement, threat or danger, adrenaline (epinephrine) is released, and a chemical message is sent to different parts of the body to activate needed responses. Too much stress, and the body operates in overdrive constantly trying to evade dangers. Too little time in the sympathetic, and the body has no time to store energy, relax, or engage in the steady work of growth.

Biologist and neurologist Robert M. Sapolsky, in *Why Zebras Don't Get Ulcers*, analyzes the effect of stress on the body's various systems.[11]

His analysis is not edifying reading. Along with epinephrine, the release of glucocorticoids (steroid hormones)—the former acting immediately and the latter more slowly—caused by constant stress is not good for the long term health of the body. Sapolsky in turn considers strokes, heart attacks, growth issues, sexual and reproductive problems, immunity, pain, memory, sleep, aging, depression, and temperament. His conclusion? Too much stress has a deleterious effect on all these systems. Living constantly in the sympathetic is bad for you.

In part, the student stress that Andy observes reflects changes in popular culture that leaves many of us more or less locked into the sympathetic nervous system. Much that pushes us into the sympathetic mode is no longer imminent threats to our lives—such as fleeing wild animals who want to eat us—but rather the psychological stresses of modern living. However, the effect is much the same. We are ready to fight off imminent threats to life and limb that largely do not exist, but our bodies behave as if they did. And rather than the sympathetic response being for a short time, many of us spend our lives there. We become ill, as the body is unable to balance itself. Many of our perceived threats are of our own making, and can mostly be averted by a change in lifestyle, one that allows us to tap more readily into the parasympathetic nervous system. It is precisely that work that Andy does in his meditation classes and workshops.

The situation that Andy's students face is compounded for children in care. Socialized in ways that easily trigger the sympathetic nervous system, children who come into care have also lived their short lives experiencing violence. Their over-developed sympathetic nervous system is locked into fight, flight or freeze. Some young girls find themselves locked into a "tend and befriend" mode, often worried sick for their younger siblings whom they have mothered. For these children, besides the "normal" social pressures that tend to switch on the sympathetic, the multiple violences they have suffered ensure they live in an agitated state. The many ailments that Sapolsky speaks of await many of these children. Loving nonviolent re-parenting, providing a safe space, a less frantic pace of life, is one way of helping traumatized children tap into the parasympathetic.

*

Casey was one of the many children we have cared for who was parentified. She was only eleven but had been the main care for her baby sister for the past eighteen months. Now the children were in different foster homes, mainly for pragmatic reasons. Casey was worried. Her response to her own trauma had been to care for little Vicki since the day she was born. Due to her young age, that care had often been inadequate. Yet, all her love had been poured into the baby. She protected her whenever possible, even putting her own person at greater risk. We were able to reassure Casey about the foster family caring for Vicki who were well-known to us. Yet while she was with us she was constantly asking permission to phone them so she could tell them how to care for Vicki.

*

In *The Body Keeps the Score*, van der Kolk attempts to answer the question: Why are some people traumatized in debilitating long-term ways, while others, who face the same or similar circumstances, find a way through to health and well-being? In short, his answer is that traumatized people have experienced difficult life events in which they suffered inescapable pain, and that this pain becomes locked in the body. Those who experience less trauma tend to have a way of escape and a network of caring relationships. When faced with inescapable shock, the human body seems to lock itself in the flight, fight, or freeze response of the autonomic nervous system. Events which appear minor to others send the traumatized person's body into overdrive. Some children seem to have a resilience which helps them to overcome trauma more easily than others. We have seen this phenomenon several times in sibling pairs.

It is beyond the scope of this short book to consider in detail van der Kolk's analysis of trauma, but his work is of direct relevance to caring for children who have experienced violence. His work confirms what we stumbled on through our experience of working with violently traumatized children, and what we had begun to practice through our study of nonviolent philosophy. Van der Kolk states, "If an organism is stuck in survival mode, its energies are focused on fighting off unseen enemies, which leaves no room for nurture, care, and love."[12] This is precisely the state in which we find many of the children we care for.

Our first experience of the "locked-in" fight or flight syndrome was with our third placement, when we were young and naive. Back in 1982 there wasn't any training in understanding the autonomic nervous system, so it took us by surprise. We had gone on vacation to our favorite farm in the lovely Lake District of northern England, where we used to hire a caravan each summer. Our two small sons loved it there. We spent the days picnicking and walking the fells. We enjoyed the quiet and safety of the camping field and farm. We had great expectations that it would be a treat for our newest foster child, who was just a little older than our boys.

The first morning the boys were playing out around the caravan. Jane suddenly called out in panic, "Where is Eddie? He was here a moment ago, and now I can't see him."

Everyone stopped and looked around. Suddenly Andy spotted a little figure running down the lane. He took off after him, eventually catching up with Eddie. The two returned, red-faced and breathless. It had been quite a run! We do not know what caused Eddie to run. His only explanation was he was going home, although he knew the drive to the Lake District had taken a couple of hours. We could only think that the sight of lakes, green fields, and farm animals had proved fearful for a child who had lived all his life surrounded by concrete. His inner panic had led him into sympathetic mode and he literally ran.

*

Kate was one of those kids who won our hearts. She was an appealing teenager whom everyone liked. Sadly, her history was one of multiple trauma, and as is often the case, she imitated the violence she had received. Often, Jane's days were interrupted by a phone call from the school saying Kate had been in yet another fight with a peer. When we talked to her about it, on each occasion there didn't seem to be a real reason. She would say, "Someone had looked at me funnily," or "I think they were talking about me." However, these occasions often led to suspension from school, and thus to consideration by the authorities about whether she needed to be in a residential setting. Unfortunately, she overheard (and misheard) her caseworker saying they were going to give her one more chance in our home. She thought she had to leave immediately. Kate took off. She ran across the road into a housing estate. Both the caseworker and Jane tried to catch her, but to no avail as she skillfully avoided them both with a speed the middle-aged found it impossible to maintain. Ultimately the caseworker called for police help in locating her. Sadly, Kate ended up being placed in the residential setting she had run to avoid. For several years, we have had occasional contact with her and lots of fond memories. We wish we could say she is doing well, but perhaps the best we can say is that she is surviving and, considering her history, maybe that is not such a bad thing.

Van der Kolk acknowledges that "Children whose parents are reliable sources of comfort and strength have a lifetime advantage—a kind of buffer against the worst that fate can hand them."[13] Children who come into care have lost that advantage, and rather have become disadvantaged through the learned helplessness of repeated acts of violence and neglect. Loving nonviolent re-parenting provides a set of relationships and a home environment where loving nonviolence is intentionally practiced to give children a safe and loving space to heal from their trauma. Our hope—anecdotally we have seen it with many of the children we have cared for—is that intentional nonviolence begins to reverse that disadvantage by providing a secure and loving base. For children whose cry for help did not register with parents and others, and for whom the violence did not stop, intentional nonviolent loving care provides the beginning of the long process of healing.

What's Your ACE Score?

In 1994, the Centers for Disease Control and Prevention, together with the health organization Kaiser Permanente, of San Diego, began to consider adverse childhood experiences (ACEs) and their effect on well-being in adulthood. The Centers for Disease Control and Prevention explained:

Specifically, the study was designed to provide data that would help answer the question: "If risk factors for disease, disability, and early mortality are not randomly distributed, what influences precede the adoption or development of them?" By providing information to answer this question, we hoped to provide scientific information that would be useful for developing new and more effective prevention programs.[14]

Between 1995 and 1997 more than 17,000 clients of Kaiser Permanente completed a confidential questionnaire about their state of health, both physical and emotional. An analysis of the results showed that the higher the level of adverse childhood experiences their respondents had suffered the more social, mental and physical health problems they encountered as adults. There is a long list of identified problems which includes: alcoholism, COPD, depression, illicit drug use, risk for intimate partner violence, smoking and adolescent pregnancy.[15]

In 2007, the original ACE survey was reduced to ten specific questions about adverse childhood experiences. Simplified, here are the ten areas that were identified; emotional abuse, physical abuse, sexual abuse, perceived oneself unloved, physical neglect, parents divorced, witnessed domestic violence, alcoholism in the home, mental illness in the home, incarcerated household member.[16]

Each one of these pinpointed by the participant is given a score of one. These are added together, so a child who has experienced five from the list will receive an ACE score of five. It is a simple, but helpful, way of determining how much trauma a child has experienced. When the survey is being taken as an adult it is important to remember that only events that happen before the participant is eighteen are relevant.

Children in foster care are very likely to have high ACE scores. When Tricia was placed with us we quickly realized she would have had an ACE score of nine. She did not answer the questions herself, but even the minimal information we were given regarding her experiences before being placed would warrant a nine. Tricia certainly reflected the severe trauma she had experienced. We must confess that there were times when we were not sure Tricia would ever be able to overcome all the hurdles in her path. Yet, slowly, she did. We cannot speak to the future, but Tricia is now in her late twenties and continues to have a good life. She has done well.

However useful the determination of ACE scores is, it is important to note that it is only a general check; a method to enable those caring for a young stranger to be realistic about responses to trauma that may occur. It is important, also, to remember that trauma and violence do not affect every child in the same way. Regardless of ACE score each child still must be treated as the individual they are. We don't want to start caring for a child with the expectation there are going to be behavioral problems just because their ACE score is high. Much better to allow it to be something we are aware of as a possibility, rather than a certainty.

Van der Kolk, who makes much of ACE scores, stresses the importance of the results. He talks about some of the findings of the original survey. In particular, he focuses on rape, alcoholism and domestic violence. He comments:

> People with an ACE score of four were seven times more likely to be alcoholic than adults with a score of zero . . . At an ACE score of zero, the prevalence of rape was 5 percent, at a score of four or more it was 33 percent.[17]

Van der Kolk notes that there have been many studies which have observed the link between those who are in abusive relationships and those who witnessed domestic violence. These findings are also very relevant to those in the role of a re-parent. We could probably say that the majority of children and teens who have come into our care have lived in homes where alcoholism and domestic violence are huge issues. In addition, many have been young victims of sexual violence.

We have seen first-hand the repeated patterns in these areas as generation after generation struggle with the same problems. Jane has sat in many meetings where the birth parents of the children we care for have been in attendance. It can be heartbreaking to listen to their tales of their own abuse and addictions. In one meeting, a mother sat in tears while her teenage sons pleaded with her to get the help she needed so they could go home. The mother was distraught. She loved her boys so much, and it was apparent to all. Yet, the many years of alcoholism and domestic violence had taken its toll on her. It was as if the abuse she had suffered first as a child and then at the hands of her partner had robbed her of all her ego strength. She wanted so badly to make a home and good life for her boys, yet she just did not have the inner resources to follow through in spite of many offers of support and help from her Department of Social Services (DSS) worker.

As re-parents it is essential that we try to see that cycle broken. On occasion, we have seen it happen where a child who was in foster care ends up as a very young mother in an abusive relationship. Nonetheless, we want to give the teenagers in our care the message that they can go on and live good and fulfilled lives. They can break the cycle of abuse and addiction.

Over the last three decades, people have become very aware of post-traumatic stress disorder (PTSD) and the debilitating effects it has on sufferers. Often it is assumed those affected by PTSD are veterans of wars, or some other traumatic event in their adult lives. The ACE studies are a means of creating awareness of the level of trauma suffered by a child. They make people aware of the correlation between trauma suffered in childhood and physical and mental conditions in later life.

We have cared for many children under the age of ten who have already suffered significant trauma. Even before reaching the age of eighteen (the study cut-off point) these children have high ACE scores, often in the 6–9 range. Loving, nonviolent re-parenting is essential to help these children begin to heal, in homes where they feel safe and secure and are not exposed to further violence. We don't want to see them victims of their backgrounds with all the ensuing problems.

*

Julie came with a history of abuse and neglect. Alcoholism was a problem in her family. Her parents and grandparents had all succumbed to its ravages. Julie was a very resilient kid. In the few years she had been with us she had already started to overcome many obstacles caused by the trauma of her background. One evening she went to a show with a group of friends. It was to be a fun night out. Unfortunately, these 18- and 19-year-olds drank large amounts of alcohol before the show. We are not sure how they obtained it! One of Julie's friends phoned us sounding really scared: "Can you come and get Julie? She tried drinking and didn't know when to stop. I think the police have been called by the theater manager."

We jumped in the car and hurried over to the theater. We arrived to see Julie slumped over a railing outside the theatre vomiting and dribbling. It was not a pretty sight! Her friends stood in a circle around her looking very scared. She was incoherent and unable to stand alone. After a quick conversation with theater staff we took her home to care for her.

Julie was not a rebellious teen. She was a sensible young woman who had graduated high school and was attending college. This pattern was repeated once more while she was still in our care, then a few times after she had moved on to live independently. Eventually, Julie, who was by this time of legal age to drink, came to the realization that she could not take alcohol safely. She knew she simply was not able to limit herself. So far, the outcome for Julie has remained a good one.

In Julie's case in addition to the trauma suffered under the age of eighteen, there was the family history of alcoholism. It should be said that half the children who have alcoholic parents will not develop a drinking problem. Nonetheless, there are significant risk factors. Studies have shown that they are four times more likely to have a problem with alcohol than people from families who do not have a problem with alcohol.[18] Scientists have debated whether there is an "alcoholic gene," without firm conclusions and the research is ongoing. The National Institute on Alcohol Abuse and Alcoholism say, "genes are responsible for about half of the risk for AUD [alcohol use disorder]."[19] They further acknowledge: "Genes alone do not determine whether someone will develop AUD. Environmental factors, as well as gene and environment interactions account for the remainder of the risk."[20]

Julie had obviously taken in this information. We had tried to give it to her gently over several months between her first incidence and leaving our care. She now recognized that, for her, drinking would lead to problems. She voiced a determination to not go the way of her family. We admired her inner strength.

We consider addiction and self-control more fully in Chapter 3.

*

We have many times pondered why children who have seen domestic violence, witnessed and experienced abuse through alcohol, had a parent in jail, been neglected, or suffered other adverse incidents repeat the pattern as they mature. We have had conversations with more than one boy who doesn't think it is worth working at school because they are convinced they will end up in jail like their father: "all the men in my family go to jail." We have fostered girls who, after leaving foster care, quickly become pregnant, have several children with various partners eventually to have their children taken into foster care. The overwhelming picture is one of a cycle of violence. It is perhaps the question we ask ourselves most often, "How do we help the kids not to succumb to following the same pattern as the generations before them."

Our aim is that loving nonviolent re-parenting will help to stop that cycle repeating. As in Julie's case we hope that the re-parenting she received during the four years she lived with us helped her to recognize that alcohol could be a problem for her and find the strength to address it.

*

Morgan and Theo were brothers. They were close in age and came to us as the result of much abuse and severe neglect. The treatment they had received in their short six and seven years of life was quite horrendous. Not only were they moved to a new home for safety reasons—and very necessary ones—it had been determined that the boys could not attend their previous school. It was too far, and the journey too long. In addition, this was one of the rare placements where the DSS did not want the parents to know the location of the children; this, too, was for their (and our) safety. They were enrolled in our local primary school.

Theo exhibited all the behaviors one sees in severely traumatized children. His first day at his new school resulted in the teacher taking Jane aside to talk about the violence he had shown toward the other children in the classroom. His mode of attack had been to try and poke all his new classmates in the eye with his pencil. On the other hand, Morgan was described as a "lovely boy," and we were told what a pleasure he was to have in class. Both boys had experienced the same abuse and neglect; they would have the same high ACE scores. The various traumas had affected them in different ways. These boys remained in foster care with us for a couple of years. The pattern never varied; Morgan continued to do well, while Theo struggled to overcome violent outbursts. We want to note again how grateful we are for the staff at many schools we have worked with. They welcome these young strangers without hesitation, often at very short notice and weather the disruption of their classes as they seek to help these traumatized children.

The story of Morgan and Theo emphasizes the importance of only seeing the ACE scores as a tool. The score is not, and should never be used as, predictive of children's violence and behavior. The score can be an aid for the re-parent, a way to foster understanding of the possible reactions from trauma.

*

In this chapter, we have discussed a few of the many trauma-based responses we have seen and how we have recognized them as such. Each story serves to illustrate the need of loving, intentionally nonviolent re-parenting for these young victims of violence. In the ensuing chapters we look in detail at four areas needing to be developed in children who have often used all their energy in merely surviving. Foster carers must deliberately nurture the psychological dispositions of empathy, self-control, reason and moral sense. We had stumbled across and named the first two of these in our experience of thirty years of working with childhood victims of trauma. We saw the lack of them and intentionally tried to help them develop. They were not only lacking in the children, but areas that we, as carers of traumatized children, needed to continue to develop. It is a lifelong process.

A few years later we discovered the further two areas of developmental need included in Steven Pinker's work,[21] and have used that as a lens for the next four chapters. Of course, none of these areas develop in isolation, but together they provide a helpful way to start to nurture the young strangers who come into our household and to create better carers for them.

Notes

1 Child Trends Data Bank, *Attitudes Toward Spanking* (Bethesda, MD: Child Trends, 2015), 2.
2 Etienne G. Krug, Linda L. Dahlberg, James A. Mercy, Anthony B. Zwi and Rafael Lozano. *World Report on Violence and Health* (Geneva: World Health Organization, 2002), 59.
3 Steven Pinker, *The Better Angels of Our Nature: How Violence Has Declined* (New York: Viking, 2011), 415.
4 World Bank, *Fertility Rate, Total (Births Per Woman)* (Washington, DC: World Bank Group, 2017), https://data.worldbank.org/indicator/SP.DYN.TFRT.IN.
5 United Cerebral Palsy and Children's Rights, "Forgotten Children: A Case for Action for Children and Youth with Disabilities in Foster Care," A Project of United Cerebral Palsy and Children's Rights (2006), www.childrensrights.org/wp-content/uploads/2008/06/forgotten_children_children_with_disabilities_in_foster_care_2006.pdf, accessed April 30, 2018.
6 June M. Clausen, John Landsverk, William Granger, David Chadwick and Alan Litrownik. "Medical Health Problems of Children in Foster Care," *Journal of Child and Family Studies*, vol. 7, no. 3 (1998), 283–296, www.researchgate.net/profile/Alan_Litrownik/publication/226139536_Mental_Health_Problems_of_Children_in_Foster_Care/links/56e34da408ae68afa10ca98f/Mental-Health-Problems-of-Children-in-Foster-Care.pdf, accessed May 2, 2018.
7 Bessel van der Kolk, *The Body Keeps the Score: Brain, Mind, and Body in the Healing of Trauma* (New York: Penguin, 2014).
8 Ibid., 32.

9 Ibid., 36.

10 Ibid., 37.

11 Robert M. Sapolsky, *Why Zebras Don't Get Ulcers* (New York: St Martin's Griffin, 2004).

12 Ibid., 76.

13 Ibid., 112.

14 The Centers for Disease Control and Prevention, "About the CDC–Kaiser ACE Study," www.cdc.gov/violenceprevention/acestudy/about.html, accessed September 10, 2018.

15 For a full list see www.cdc.gov/violenceprevention/acestudy/about.html.

16 To read the complete questions see Carol Redding, "The Adverse Childhood Experiences Study: Springboard to Hope," www.acestudy.org/the-ace-score.html, accessed February 7, 2018.

17 Van der Kolk, *The Body Keeps Score*, 148–149.

18 NIH, "A Family History of Alcoholism," National Institute on Alcohol Abuse and Alcoholism, https://pubs.niaaa.nih.gov/publications/familyhistory/famhist.htm, accessed February 19, 2018.

19 NIH, "Genetics of Alcohol Use Disorder," www.niaaa.nih.gov/alcohol-health/overview-alcohol-consumption/alcohol-use-disorders/genetics-alcohol-use-disorders, accessed February 21, 2018.

20 Ibid.

21 See Chapter 2 for details.

2 Nurturing Our Better Angel of Empathy

Carlie was a teenager who had problems with electronics, in particular, her phone and Xbox Live, where she met new people to chat with. In conjunction with the caseworker we had suggested she restricted the hours she used it. However, that wasn't a success as it just pushed her to lie about her usage. In all other respects, Carlie was an easy teen to have in the house.

We were going on vacation. It had been a grueling year and we needed a rest. We wanted to spend some time with our son and daughter-in-law. Carlie was going to stay with a pleasant couple who were also foster carers. She was very familiar with them as we often cared for each other's children. Carlie liked going there and was happy to stay with them so she could continue with her summer job. Confident she would be well cared for, we headed south.

A few nights later we received a frantic call from them. Carlie was missing! They had followed the correct procedure and notified all the appropriate authorities. We felt really sorry that this had happened as we knew, first-hand, how much trouble it is when a child absconds.

Happily, Carlie was found a couple of days later safe and sound, although as a runaway who was in foster care a warrant had been issued and a court appearance ensued. The story unfolded that she had gone to meet a girl she had met online who lived in another state. She had used some of her savings to purchase a bus ticket. Her plan seemed somewhat vague and the story kept changing. However, the best we could glean was that her idea had been to have a few days of fun then return to the other family before we arrived home. Carlie thought they wouldn't tell us she had been missing!

When asked whether she had considered all the people, including her birth parents, who would be worried, she could not grasp why people would care. When told that her escapade had probably cost thousands of dollars in terms of DSS, police, lawyers, court, she shrugged and said people were stupid to have involved all those agencies. Clearly Carlie had no empathy for the worry caused, nor had she any grasp of how unsafe her actions were.

*

On Monday, March 4, 1861, the newly elected President of the United States, Abraham Lincoln, gave his first inaugural address. Between his election victory in the previous November and the day of his swearing in, seven southern states had seceded from the Union. To say the least, Lincoln's speech was written at one the most difficult times for the United States—the verge of civil war. Lincoln could not predict the grim future that ensued, but tried, nonetheless, to prevent the possibility of violence. He addressed his conciliatory words mostly to those in the south, calling them "not enemies, but friends." His hope was that their shared memories and experiences would again be touched by "the better angels of our nature."[1] In other words, Lincoln appealed to the higher impulses, drives, and intuitions of his hearers—their better angels—urging them to forsake the demons of hatred and violence. The civil war was to claim the lives of 620,000 Americans in a brutal conflict that presaged the later wars of the twentieth century, when 203 million people were killed in war and as a direct result of war.[2] Humanity, it seems, still struggles to find its better angels.

Nonetheless, psychologist Steven Pinker chose Lincoln's memorable phrase for the title of his 2011 book *The Better Angels of Our Nature: Why Violence Has Declined.*[3] His argument, contentious in some circles, is that despite the appalling death toll and human propensity to harm, violent actions—as measured by number of incidences per 100,000 of the population—have been in decline for, more or less, the last 500 years. Even the appalling number of war deaths in the twentieth century accounted for only 3.5 percent of all deaths, compared with 15 percent in tribal pre-state societies.[4] Pinker's is a hopeful account, and his suggestion is that humanity has steadily been discovering its better angels, which he defines as "the psychological faculties that steer us away from violence, and whose increased engagement over time can be credited for the decline in violence."[5] For Pinker, these better angels amount to empathy, self-control, moral sense, and reason. By developing our better angels in these four areas, Pinker argues that our common future will be less violent than our past.

As we considered how we may best represent the re-parenting of children who have been victims of violence we pondered Pinker's "better angels." If the development of these human faculties over the last 500 years is responsible for a steady reduction of violence, then it seems likely that the development of these faculties by re-parents, and the modeling of these faculties to traumatized children, would be a vital part of the strategy of intentional loving nonviolence. What difference would it make in the lives of traumatized children if their carers developed empathy, self-control, moral sense, and reason? Would re-parents who modelled these dispositions help their children grow in these ways too? Doubtless, buried in our collective psyche remain other better angels to be uncovered, but these four at least give us a place to start. In this and the three subsequent chapters we will consider in turn empathy, self-control, moral sense, and reason, and how each of these plays into the loving nonviolent care of children.

In our strategy to help foster carers become loving nonviolent re-parents, we begin with our better angel of empathy. In the most general terms, it's easy to imagine that a more empathic world will be a less violent world. More empathic parenting will mean fewer violent homes, and, likely, fewer children in care. Empathic re-parenting of children taken into care will provide a safe place where children can begin to find healing from their trauma.

Empathy for those who are like us is an easy reach. It becomes more difficult when we face differences, when our worlds are unalike, and when to put yourself in someone else's shoes is a tight fit, or no fit at all. In this chapter, then, we look at the complexity of re-parenting in a diverse world, and how differences in social class, race, gender, and religion play into loving nonviolent relationships.

Empathy is a somewhat in-vogue idea. First used in 1909 by British psychologist Edward Bradford Titchener to translate the German word *Einfürlung,*[6] empathy in general usage means the capacity to understand how another feels, and in some way to share those feelings. Though only coined in English at the beginning of the twentieth century, the concept was older in Germany, and was in Britain by a different name. In Chapter 4 we look at moral sense and how, according to eighteenth-century Scottish philosophers Adam Smith and David Hume, moral sense is rooted in the natural human capacity of sympathy. It is clear when reading these giants of the Enlightenment, that, for them, sympathy is very similar to the way we describe empathy today. Yet, not all have agreed. Historically, philosophers have considered the mind and rationality of greater importance than sympathy, or empathy, which is emotional, sentimental, and hence less trustworthy. Without a doubt, reason is important. It counts as one of Steven Pinker's "better angels," and we include it in Chapter 5, as one of the four psychological faculties that have helped humanity steer away from violence. Nonetheless, to think of emotion—or the passions as they used to call them—as morally helpful has been a minority position in philosophical thought. Thankfully, today's philosophers and psychologists are generally agreed that thinking and feeling, reason and empathy play equal parts in helping us shape a good life.

In this more holistic perspective, we have been helped greatly by the work of primatologists, and other ethologists such as Frans de Waal. Historically, animals have fared poorly when compared to human beings. Being perceived as without rationality the animal is naturally aggressive and violent. Survival of the fittest has often been taken as survival of the most ruthless. When humans exercise violence it is the outworking of the "animal nature" that we share with the lower animals, the savage beasts. "You're such an animal!" has never been a compliment. In religious accounts, humans, created in the image of God, had souls in a way that animals did not, thus differentiating them from animals.

For philosophers such as René Descartes, it was a reasonable soul that separated humans from animals. Reason was our redeeming feature. He argued that even the dullest human being could use speech, even in an elementary way that no animals could. For Descartes this demonstrated a property—a reasonable soul—that no animal possessed. Animals were merely machines.

When a human cried out in pain it was because of a reasonable soul. However, when an animal similarly cried out in pain, it was mere appearance as the animal's cry was the function of a machine and not a soul.[7]

The gulf between humans and animals was thus fixed, and even those who have never heard of Descartes's theory have been shaped by it. This understanding is the basis of what philosopher Peter Singer terms "speciesism," which he defines as "a prejudice or attitude of bias in favor of the interests of one's own species against those of members of other species."[8] It is on the basis of speciesism that the human animal has enacted all manner of horrors against other animals. To add further insult to injury, we have assumed that aggression belongs to the animal, and insofar as a human is aggressive he is acting out of the animal nature. When a human acts with kindness, compassion, or empathy, she does so out of the uniquely human reasonable soul.

Contemporary ethologists have challenged this false division between humans and animals. Frans de Waal and others have demonstrated that animals are not only, or always, aggressive, but have extraordinary potential for empathy. The human capacity for aggression and empathy is, then, much the same as for other animals, and de Waal presents ample evidence that the human empathic response is as natural and animalistic as the aggressive response. After a thorough investigation of primate and other animal behavior, together with its corresponding human behavior, he concludes that the "animals are merely aggressive to selfish ends" narrative is equally false for both humans and other animals. He asks:

> Why did natural selection design our brains so that we're in tune with our fellow human beings, feeling distress at their distress and pleasure at their pleasure? If exploitation of others were all that mattered, evolution should never have gotten into the empathy business.[9]

A growing consensus is that survival of the fittest is not as much about aggressive takeovers as it is about cooperation. Humanity has prevailed precisely because human beings, as social animals, learned successfully to care for their young and for each other.

Economist and social theorist Jeremy Rifkin popularized the work of ethologists, psychologists, and others on empathy in his *The Empathic Civilization*. He comments:

> Recent discoveries in brain science and child development are forcing us to rethink the long-held belief that human beings are, by nature, aggressive, materialistic, utilitarian, and self-interested. The dawning realization that we are a fundamentally empathic species has profound and far-reaching consequences for society.[10]

Despite religious apocalypticism and media hype that the world is terrible and getting worse, Rifkin argues, "Although life as it's lived on the ground, close to home, is peppered with suffering, stresses, injustices, and foul play, it is, for the most part, lived out in hundreds of small acts of kindness and generosity."[11] In other words, human nature is empathic. Rifkin demonstrates his argument using the change in psychology from the Freudian understanding of human nature as aggressive—driven by libidinal and thanotic needs—to an understanding of human nature in which relationality is paramount.[12] He calls this *homo empathicus*.[13]

For our purposes, empathy is necessary for the human animal's moral commitment to the principle that is nonviolence, and especially for the loving nonviolent re-parenting of children who have already suffered too much violence.

Empathy in a Diverse World

In *Welcoming Strangers*, we expanded an understanding of violence to include psychological and systemic harm, as well as more obvious physical and sexual injuries. The children we care for have, as often as not, suffered from violence in all these diverse ways. In this chapter, we explore more thoroughly the prejudice and discrimination that children of color and differently gendered children face, and the psychological and systemic violence that often accompany it. When children are taken from their birth family, even for a very good reason, we have suggested that such a breaking of the ties of attachment is a form of violence. That violent dislocation is all the more intense when a child is removed from her culture and placed in an alien one. For children in care, this is often their reality.

It's important to lay our cards on the table: we are socially middle-class, white, cisgender, heterosexuals, British by upbringing, and from a culturally Christian tradition. In most respects that makes us part of the dominant culture, with all of the privilege, and often unrecognized prejudice, that includes. Our upbringing was in a largely white, heteronormative, middle-class society. In the England of our childhood, our neighborhoods, schools, and social groups were exclusively white, though Andy recalls one brown student from India in his high school, whose parents were medical doctors. In other words, unconsciously we viewed the world from the lofty heights of white normativity. People of color did not feature in our lives.

However, we did grow up in the shadow of a fading empire, and people of color were on the margins of our consciousness—relics of empire, people once conquered. In the 1960s, Britain faced its first waves of immigrants from the former colonies, but not to the neighborhoods in which we were raised. This did not mean we were free from prejudice. In our childhood the Irish, Jewish, German, and French all received more than a share of mockery and ridicule. We were raised in the milieu of the "tight Jew," the "thick Irish," and the "dirty Arab." Such prejudice was never at the forefront of social discourse, but always in the background. Xenophobia is a function of most social groups.

In England, all but one of the children we cared for were white. The exception was one mixed-race child whose mother tried to hide that fact from her child (see Clare's story below). When we began foster care in the United Kingdom in the 1980s, agencies were very clear that children of color ought to be fostered by families of color. Children of Pakistani or Caribbean origin would be helped most by families who understood their culture and religion.

In the United States our experience has been different. The latest data at the time of writing show that our small city, population 30,720, is 64.3 percent white. The next largest group is Asian at 16.8 percent, with 7.3 percent Hispanic, 6.4 percent Black, 5.1 percent mixed race, 0.3 percent American Indian and a tiny 0.1 percent other races.[14] Historically our city is friendly to the LQBTQ+ community. It was identified as one of the "fabulous gay-friendly" cities in which to live in a book of that title.[15]

Contra to our experience in England, our current fostering agency has no emphasis on children being placed with culturally, racially, or religiously similar families. Hence, we have cared for black, Latinx, and mixed-race children. We have never cared for Asian, or Muslim, children. Most of the children we have cared for came from a socially and economically poor background, with a few rare exceptions. We have cared, too, for gay and trans children.

When children have entered our home they invariably have faced a cultural disconnect. Though this is most clear with children of color, it is also reality for children raised in poverty. We have been aware that our values are largely traditional middle-class values, where a premium is placed on honesty, truth telling, hard work, respect for adults, respect for others' property, social manners, and such like. In chaotic homes where truth telling will likely involve receiving a "good" spanking from an adult, telling lies, in the vain hope of escaping a beating, is a useful strategy and is learned early. In families where food is scarce and "stuff" rare, why not take what belongs to others if you get the chance? Children socialized in a world of doing whatever it takes to avoid pain and survive take time to adjust to middle-class sensibilities.

Our lifestyle is culturally British. All children we have cared for in the United States come to our home as strangers; they to us, and we to them. We talk differently, use strange words and phrases, and we prepare food differently. Though we have lived in the United States for 23 years, and are naturalized U.S. citizens, in many respects we are "un-American." We are just different. Add to all the above that our home is vegetarian, with no meat products, and most children experience a cultural shock to varying degrees.

Though most people assume that the United Kingdom and the United States share much in common, beside the political "special relationship," and the pervasive hegemony of the American TV and movie industries, we still experienced massive disorientation when we first moved to the

United States. Everything was different, the food, the people, the attitudes, the language, the driving, the humor, the school system, and, to cap it all, the doors open on the "wrong" side! We missed, even yearned for, the familiar. Sometimes it was like a physical ache. Even so, we were in the United States by choice. We hadn't been forced to leave our home. Our experience helps us empathize with the children we care for; they too are in an unfamiliar situation, but not out of choice.

*

"I've never had sheets on a bed before."

"I get a toothbrush of my own? Why do you want me to clean my teeth every day?"

"Why do I have to go to bed? I just stay up until I fall asleep on the couch."

"We always watch that program. Why won't you let me?"

"I have to tell you if I'm going out? Why?"

"I want my blanket. It has a special smell."

"Can you leave the light on. I'm scared. It's so quiet here at night."

"Can you make mac 'n' cheese out of a box? Not the home-made stuff."

"I saw a cow. A real cow! I only saw one in a book before."

*

The unavoidable truth, then, is that the violent dislocation and disruption children experience when taken from their birth families is compounded when placed in our home (or placed in any other foster home). It is necessary to face this unpleasant reality before the healing from violence induced trauma can take place.

Race Matters

After Barack Obama was elected President of the United States in 2008, there was much talk that we had, at last, entered a "post-racial society," and that in such a society we were now "color-blind." The proof of such was the election of a black president. Despite the huge gains in racial equality that Obama's election demonstrated, the reality that we are now "post-racial" has proved not to be so sanguine.[16] Hate crimes continue. Black parents still tell their children to be careful around white cops. And, perhaps most telling of all, barely hidden racism was a feature in the election of Donald Trump as President. Does this mean that the United States is on the verge of undoing the good work of civil rights, and that all along Americans have been basically racist? Probably not. In the not too distant past, riots against African Americans and lynchings were a feature of the American landscape. In the 1880s, around 150 black men were lynched each year. The number began to fall by the turn of the twentieth century and fell dramatically by the 1940s, to virtually zero. Today, lynchings are a lesson in the progress we have made for civics classes.[17] Actual homicides based on racial hatred, according to the FBI, have rarely been above five per year since data were first collected in 1996, the year 2016 being an outlier with nine.[18] The change shows massive progress. However, the over 5,000 hate crimes reported by the FBI for 2016 is still too many, with more progress to be made. We live with the legacy of a tragically and deeply racist past, and its shadow extends into the present.

On March 1, 2015 the British Sunday newspaper *The Observer* announced in a headline "Why Racism is Not Backed by Science."[19] Science writer Adam Rutherford helpfully summarized the current standing of race among geneticists. He comments:

> We now know that the way we talk about race has no scientific valid- ity. There is no genetic basis that corresponds with any particular group of people, no essential DNA for black people or white people or any- one. This is not a hippy ideal. It is a fact.

He concludes, "race does not exist; racism does." His article, like others of its ilk, bring to a wider audience the findings of science, and that science tells us that there is no scientific, biological, or genetic reason to divide humanity into races. This is good news, and gives us a basis to make progress.

However, things exist in ways other than by scientific proof. In the social sciences, it has been common since the mid-1960s, to speak of the social con- struction of reality.[20] In brief, as people interact in social systems, over time the representation of each other's ways of thinking and acting becomes for- malized in institutions. So, the biological fact that race has no scientific basis does not necessarily mean that race does not exist. Since philosophers in the eighteenth century began to classify humanity on the basis of the color of skin, and that each such grouping had certain psychological characteristics, the idea of race began to be institutionalized in human interactions. The institutionalizing of race meant that each racial group was given a certain standing in society, and people began to act as if race was in fact a natural reality. Whites were the superior race, blacks the most inferior, with Asians and native peoples in between. It is tempting to say, as Rutherford did in his newspaper article, that race does not exist; it is merely a social construction, as if social constructions of reality do not really count. The unfortunate truth is that when people act within their social construction of reality its effects are all too real in the everyday world. People do believe that their race, national- ity, religion, or gender is superior and act accordingly. Other people suffer.

On June 17, 2015, a young white man entered the Emanuel AME church in Charleston, South Carolina, seemingly joined in the prayer meeting, and then killed nine people, including the pastor. Those he murdered were all black. The white man had associations with white supremacy groups. These brutal racist murders sent shock waves of grief, and anger, through the nation. The following Sunday, Andy wrote a blog in solidarity with the black community: "Today I am Black Too." The picture heading the blog was of Andy and one of our African American children with arms around each other, smiling, at a festival where our foster son had been performing. Reading the blog through again, it expressed what we wanted to say about being an ally, so we include parts of it here:

> I was deeply saddened this week by the murders of nine Black people at prayer by a racist, white supremacist. Perhaps a poor admission, but I was not surprised by the murders. There has been too much violence against my Black brothers and sisters to be surprised by another act of violence. Nor do I consider the event "unspeakable" or "unthinkable," for in truth racism is a reality and we must speak about it and think about it. I read much media commentary from the mainstream to the blogs. Some were deeply moving. Some insightful. However, I was not impressed by those who wanted to make this about gun control, or by those who made much of an attack on Christianity, or by those who rushed too quickly to pronounce the killer mentally ill, and therefore beyond responsibility. Those analyses diverted attention from the painful issue we would rather not face. Racism is alive and well, and can have terrible consequences.
>
> However, racism is unsustainable, and I am ultimately optimistic. Here's why.
>
> The house that is racism has a top beam to its frame too heavy for its supporting pillars. The ideological pillars that support racism are: first, that race has some essential basis in biology or genetics, and second, that having made the distinction between races, some are superior to others, and that one "White" is superior to all. These pillars are too weak to support the top beam of racism, and racism must inevitably collapse—just as the sexist ideology that males are naturally superior to females is collapsing, and the ideology that straight is superior to gay is rapidly disintegrating.
>
> For the best part of a couple of centuries, in western culture we have bought the lie that race is based in biology and is an essential basis for dividing humanity into different races. I am persuaded by political philosopher Charles Mills careful work in demonstrating that race, as it has been understood, is a product of the modern period. The ideology of racism was constructed as a way of justifying the dominance of White western nations in their bid for world dominance. Race was established for social and economic reasons. If you can find good reasons why people of other places are inferior to you, then why not take their land, their resources, kill them if necessary, or else enslave them to do your work? A convenient categorization was the color of skin, and many of the West's most notable thinkers (such as German philosopher Immanuel Kant) engaged in the construction of an ideology that allowed the domination of some by others. Race is a construction of the way physical characteristics are given social meaning . . .

Science has exposed the lie of this ideology. Race has no scientific basis. There are no genetic racial differences. Differences occur as a response to environment. Race is, therefore, biologically meaningless.

It is tempting, then, to say that, therefore, we can now dispense with talk about race. The trouble is, that while race is not a meaningful way to characterize human beings, culturally mistaken views of race and racism are still very powerful. Race is a myth. But myths may be thought of in two ways: first, as something that is untrue and has no basis in reality, and second, as a way of telling a story that gives sense to life. Race is a myth in both ways. Scientifically it is untrue and has no basis in reality. But the way race has been constructed and the stories told about race make for powerful story-telling. "You rape our women" and "You're stealing our country" are powerful invocations of a strong and enduring cultural myth.

. . .

Ultimately, racism, based on its faulty pillars of genetics and superiority is unsustainable. Events, such as that we saw this week, will doubtless continue. In the long term, in solidarity, with good will, education, generosity and love we can leave racism behind.[21]

Andy's blog was written in solidarity with African Americans. Even so, some progressive white friends criticized the sentiment as a white man trying to appropriate black identity and struggles. (My black friends thanked me for the blog.) The criticism was aimed mostly at the blog's title: "Today I am Black Too." How could Andy possibly know what it feels like to be a black person in America? How could he know the fear that Charleston created? In part, the criticism was justified. However, Andy was not making any kind of ontological or existential claim about blackness. Rather, he was using the same rhetorical device that John F. Kennedy did when he said, "Ich bin ein Berliner," on June 26, 1963, in a speech in West Berlin. For Kennedy, it is an empathic sign of solidarity with Berliners who had lived in a divided city under the shadow of Soviet Communism. It was that sense Andy had intended. It speaks of being an ally. But, the response to Andy's blog highlights the difficulties we face when we take on the necessary task of becoming allies in solidarity with those who suffer prejudice and discrimination.

Do we still, then, need to take notice of race? Surely, the world would be better if we took no notice of the color of someone's skin and accepted all equally regardless of race? Such is a noble sentiment, and might be considered one of society's highest goals. However, to pretend that we are even close to achieving that is unhelpful. Despite Obama's eight years in office, incidences of racially motivated violence, structural and institutional racism, and open discrimination still exist. In 2018, a movement such as Black Lives Matter still makes sense. Our social reality is that race has so shaped much

of private and public life, to the detriment of people of color, that to pretend race doesn't matter is to ignore historic and present injustices. At the
same time, the moral imperative to treat all equally, toward which "color-
blind" points, remains. To nurture successfully the children placed with us
we need to be "color aware." We must be able to affirm each child's past
and that includes the color of their skin, with all its associations for good
and ill. We endeavor to make each child feel valued for who they are, not
what they look like. We need to help children and teens find a strong self-
identity. Yet we recognize that sadly, racism and prejudice exist and, especially
with darker skinned children, part of nurturing them is teaching them how
to be safe and what to do when they encounter prejudice.

*

It was summer time, and we had spent a pleasurable couple of weeks in the
north of England reconnecting with family and friends. Now, sadly, Andy
had to leave. University commitments had dictated the date he needed to
return to the States. However, Jane was staying on for an extra few days
to attend her niece's marriage ceremony. The wedding day dawned bright
and sunny, and an excellent day of celebration was enjoyed by all. Jane
was pleased to have shared in this important day with the opportunity to
luxuriate in the lavish reception with her mother and two sisters. Photos
of the day find four happy women sharing uncommon moments together.
To outsiders (including Andy) the "Hall girls" bear remarkable similarities. Said one guest, "Well, you can tell you are all related"; and another,
"Strong family likeness there"; with a third, "Don't you girls all take after
your mum?"

Of course, the perception of mother and daughters is that they don't look
alike at all! Jane can see some family similarities, but not too many. Physical
traits that make for a family resemblance seem obvious to others, but not to
the family. Truth be told, no one would mistake one for the other. Jane was
dark haired as a child, while her two sisters had been blondes. Now they all
need a little help from the hairdresser! Yet, at the wedding, people, some
who had known the four women for years, and some who were strangers,
were all commenting that they were easily recognizable as family. How
important, then, is physical likeness?

*

A question for every potential foster carer or adoptive parent is: does it matter that the child doesn't look like me? To be sure, as with the Hall girls,
physical likeness, like beauty, can be in the eye of the beholder. People see a
bunch of children and make assumptions. One year we took six children—
three boys and three girls—on a camping vacation to the beautiful Vendée
region in France, staying a few nights each in Saint-Jean-de-Mont and
Saint-Giles-Croix-de-Vie. Our youngest was about 14 months, the eldest 12 years old, with a spread in between. The north of England to the

mid-Atlantic coast of France necessitated an overnight stop both ways. We had a wonderful time creating lots of happy memories. If we close our eyes it's easy to imagine the taste of the fresh warm baguettes in the morning, and the warmth of the Vendée sands between our toes. On our return home, we stayed overnight at a quaint little hotel in the small English coastal town of Folkestone. In the hotel lounge during a pre-dinner drink, a couple who were seated nearby struck up a conversation, and asked about our vacation. The children happily recited their individual highlights. Complimenting the children on their manners and behavior—always nice for foster carers to hear—the man turned to us and said, "Your kids all look so alike." We simply smiled, quietly amused. Afterward we wondered what the man would have thought if we had told him that between them this clutch of kids had four fathers and three mothers! Physical likeness can be illusory.

Even so, it remains true that families often do share many characteristics. Despite the trick of the eyes and assumptions people sometimes make, family resemblance is often not even close within foster families. We have cared for children who are white, black, Latinx, and mixed race; though to date we have not had any Asian children. To be a foster carer means that we take children who often do not look like us. We were delighted recently to meet an Asian foster family caring for a white baby. To care for these children in the most loving way requires empathic re-parenting skills, seeking to understand and feel sympathy with their varied experiences and backgrounds.

But, it's not always easy to do. One white foster parent told us that her black friend had advised her that it was unwise to let her thirteen-year-old mixed-race foster son go out at dusk to a neighboring friend's house wearing a hoodie with the hood pulled up. From the friend's experience with her own children, people too quickly made assumptions about black kids in hoodies making trouble. The child in foster care was a gentle teenager who had never been in any trouble. Yet, issues arose because of his dark skin and racist assumptions. The friend's advice was better to be safe than sorry.

*

Our own African American foster son was visiting extended birth family in the South for a few weeks; a visit approved and arranged by DSS. Arriving back at the Greyhound bus station, he told us excitedly that he had witnessed a store being robbed while shopping at a strip mall. He thought the police may have thought he was involved simply because he was black. He was scared and ran away from the scene as fast as he could. That night the story had featured on the local TV news, together with aerial footage of the mall. The broadcaster said, "Police are anxious to interview a black teenager seen running from the scene of the crime." Our foster son was sure this was him, but he did not go forward for interview. Teenagers love drama, and this story may well have been exaggerated. Nevertheless, it illustrates that this young man was very aware that he could become a suspect in a crime simply because of his skin color.

*

Ricardo, a Latino boy, was completely aware of his good looks. He loved clothes, was very fashion conscious, and was always immaculately turned out, down to his spotless matching shoes. He loved to go shopping with us, especially at his favorite clothes chain store, where designer labels are sold at a discount. Ricardo had an after-school job at a fast food chain, mainly so he could indulge his love of clothes and shoes. We were happy that he liked to spend his money on extra clothes—much healthier than drugs and alcohol!

On a dull, overcast Saturday afternoon we decided to take a trip to the store.

"Jane, Andy, look what I have found in the clearance section. It is only $10. Isn't it awesome? I'll look so cool in it."

Ricardo held up a fashionable suit, baggy pants, zip-up top, in pure white. It had fancy trimming on the cuffs and neckline. The suit had been expensive, but with several reduction stickers piled on top of each other, it had obviously been difficult to sell. The drastic price cut didn't surprise us, as the color was so impractical. But not for Ricardo, who was excited with his find.

"It is not the best color," Jane warned, trying gently to dissuade him, thinking about laundry. "I think you'll find the pants will get dirty around the ankles very quickly."

Ricardo's face fell.

"Still, for $10 it's great, even just the top is worth it," remarked Andy, taking a cue from Ricardo's expression and trying to save the situation. "Great find!"

"Well, it certainly looks your style. You will look very cool in it," Jane added, not wanting to dampen Ricardo's enthusiasm.

We proceeded to the checkout. Ricardo stood in front of us still chattering excitedly planning which shoes and T-shirt would look best with his new find. The line was long, but he eventually reached the young woman assistant at the checkout. We stood back watching. The assistant looked at the price tag, then looked at Ricardo, then looked back at the price tag. We could see her mind working as she glanced between dark-skinned teen and price tag with several stickers on it. She looked disdainfully at him and said, "I need to call the manager."

Andy, taking in the situation quickly, stepped forward, "Is there a problem with my son's purchase?" The shop assistant, embarrassed, immediately changed her attitude, and somewhat red-faced said, "Oh no, sir!" She rang up the clothing, but she, Ricardo, and we, were not fooled by the hasty cover-up.

In helping our teens learn responsibility, our policy has always been to help them shop wisely, sometimes letting them make silly mistakes (as with the white suit). This has included learning to look at bargain racks and waiting for things to come on sale. So Ricardo's bargain find was not unusual in our household, and over the years, we have taken many teens to buy clothes and sundry items in the same store. To date none of our white foster children have ever been questioned when they have presented items that have been reduced multiple times.

*

Not only have we cared for children who don't look like us, we have had children who don't look like each other, even siblings.

Jane answered the phone, "Hi Jane!" said the long-suffering caseworker, "We were wondering if you could take a brother and sister. The little boy is six, and his sister is nine." We had a quick conversation and happily agreed to take the children into our home. The caseworker arrived a couple of hours later. She escorted two bemused children from the car, each clutching a little carrier bag of their few and tattered belongings.

"This is Johnnie," the caseworker said, pointing to the very fair-skinned, blonde little boy. "And this is Clare," she added, indicating the petite, brown-eyed, black-haired girl.

We welcomed the children and went into the usual routine of making them feel as safe as we could, despite their bewilderment.

Over a cup of tea, the caseworker gave us the little history she had. The children had been removed from their home because their mother was unable to care for them due to her addiction to alcohol. Their mother loved the children and had done her best to care for them. Unfortunately, the best efforts of DSS to keep the kids in their home had failed and the time had come when the agency no longer felt that the children were safe.

"I'm really worried about Clare," the caseworker continued. "She has no self-esteem, and really no self-identity."

"Is that a result of going to school dirty and unkempt? I know that can be really hard on kids. Or is there any special reason, as you have mentioned it?" Andy asked.

"Yes, there is a special reason. It is really sad, actually. As you will have noticed, Clare is mixed race, however her mother didn't want her to know this. She has never let her look in any mirrors, and if the child asked why her skin is darker than her brother's she was just told she was sunburnt."

"Poor girl," responded Andy. "She has really been made to feel the color of her skin is shameful."

"Exactly, I hope you can help her. Anyway, I must go. Phone me if you need anything." The caseworker took her leave and we began the task of caring.

The question on our lips for the next few weeks was how we could nurture Clare. She felt herself totally worthless, and constantly talked about wanting to know her father's name and meeting him. This was not a possibility as her mother did not know who he was; or at least, that was her claim.

In reality, Clare was a really pretty and appealing little girl, and always received lots of compliments whenever we were out and about. In the year

Clare was with us, we grew very fond of her and still cherish the good memories. For that year, we did everything we could to help her be successful, and to find her self-identity.

It was not enough. Clare continued to have problems, especially at school. She was unable to make friends or function with peers, and had no relationship with her little brother. The two were unable to bond. Eventually it was suggested that Clare needed to go to a residential facility to get further help with her problems.

We don't know what the long-term outcome was for Clare. We heard through the grapevine that she had a lengthy stay in her residential placement where work was done to reunite Clare and her mother. She returned home, but became pregnant as a very young teenager, such was her need for love and identity. After that, we lost touch completely. As we write, Clare will now be in her thirties.

*

As foster carers, we had a lot to learn about nurturing black children. We learned to ask for help from black friends, and have been willing to take their advice. We have never been shunned by them or made to feel inadequate. Black friends have always seemed to appreciate that we have tried not to make the children in our care "white."

Jane had taken Darius to the pediatrician for his routine check. In our state, every child in foster care must be checked by a pediatrician within thirty days of placement. Jane returned home and pronounced Darius healthy and now up-to-date with all his immunizations.

"There was one thing though. The doctor said his scalp is dry. She suggested we oil it."

"Do you know what that means? What sort of oil? How much oil?" questioned Andy.

"I'm not really sure. I thought I'd ask one of my black colleagues at work tomorrow."

"Good idea, we want to ensure we do it right."

Jane asked and was instructed in the art of caring for his hair. We were also given advice about which were the best products to use and where to purchase them. It is almost embarrassing to confess that we had never considered that different hair types required different treatment. We were happy to learn.

Many years later we had another learning curve about hair. We had a fourteen-year-old white boy in our care when we were asked if we could take a similar aged African American boy. Due to the first boy being from a background steeped in racism, we hesitated momentarily, but decided to take the second boy. We need not have worried. Tyler and Deonte quickly became fast friends. A few weeks later they wanted (and needed) haircuts. We made an appointment at our usual hairdressers. They had cut Tyler's hair many times and he had been happy with the result.

"Will they get my line right?" Deonte queried. "They must get my line right or I'll look stupid. They'll laugh at me at school."

"I'm sure they will. Michael is very skilled. We have taken lots of kids to him and they have always been okay."

"Yes," added Tyler. "He's really cool."

"But will he know how to do a line?" Deonte persisted worriedly.

"You just tell him exactly what you want and we are sure it will be fine." We tried to reassure him. "And, if it is not right we can always go somewhere else."

We didn't really understand what the "line" was, but in nurturing Deonte we were determined that he would feel good about himself.

After his hair had been cut we thought his hair really looked nice. To our eyes, it seemed our hairdresser had done exactly what Deonte had asked for. But no!

"I really liked him, but he hasn't got the line right," Deonte wailed. "It's not right. What shall I do?"

We assured Deonte we would investigate where he could get the "line" corrected. So back to colleagues for more advice. We were given the name of a barber who specialized in African American hair. It was just a small place, and we had passed it many times but never noticed the obscure doorway between two shops that led to an upper room. The two guys who ran it were great fun. We learnt what the line was (top of the forehead at the hairline). We also learnt that Deonte should return every couple of weeks between haircuts to have the "line" neatened for a nominal charge. Deonte was happy; Tyler, too, insisted that he would no longer go anywhere else for his haircut.

We were impressed by the tiny place, always full of black teenage boys. The two men running it did all they could to encourage the boys (and not just ours) to do well at school, to be respectful to adults and to help around the house. They even asked kids to bring in copies of their report cards and other achievements. These emblazoned the walls.

It may seem that hair style is an insignificant thing, although, perhaps, not so much for a fourteen-year-old! It is these small things that are important in nurturing strangers. After the years of neglect and abuse that many have suffered, these teenagers need to feel valued for who they are.

So we try to find ways to appreciate their race and heritage and give the message that it is important to us as well as them. Sometimes it is through something really simple. We remember the smile on the face of a Latina young woman when Jane found Puerto Rican bread in a grocery store and bought it for everyone to eat at dinner. She was delighted and eager that we would all like it.

Empathic re-parenting won't necessarily protect these children and teenagers from the racism they will encounter in society. Part of caring will, then, of necessity, include frank conversations designed to help the kids find ways to be safe. However, empathic re-parenting can teach them to have pride in their heritage and give them the message that they are valued and cared for.

Gender Fluidity

In the 1980s and early 1990s, there was little awareness that children in care might face gender identity issues, and we confess that we did not have, then, much experience of re-parenting teenagers who identify as gay or transgender. It's likely that some of our kids were gay, but, like most people then, we were unaware of gender possibilities. Since then, we have provided a home for a couple of transgender teenagers, a few openly gay kids, and one or two who were questioning their gender identity.

Perhaps, it is important to clarify that none of these teenagers were in foster care because of gender issues. They had suffered violence with its ensuing trauma, and high ACE scores in common with many other teenagers we have cared for. However, each of these young people had faced some additional problems over their gender issues. For a teenager already struggling with rejection from their family (real or perceived) this compounds their trauma. Even so, cultural mores are slowly changing, and gay and transgender kids find much more acceptance in schools than even ten years ago.

Yet change comes slowly, and the teens we cared for had all experienced prejudice at some level. The transgender and gay teenagers we cared for all came to us between the ages of thirteen and sixteen, a tough age for all kids as they move from childhood toward adulthood with the ensuing struggle for identity. We found it a particularly hard time for the transgender teens.

Psychologist and clinical social worker Elijah C. Nealy has worked extensively with lesbian, gay, bisexual and transgender teenagers. He talks about the struggle transgender teens face at puberty. His knowledge helps in our attempts to be empathic re-parents to transgender teens. In the same way, we consulted friends to help us be better re-parents to black and bi-racial children we reached out to, mainly through reading, to equip ourselves to re-parent trans-teens. We wish Nealy's book had been published when we had our first experience of a transgender thirteen-year-old.

Nealy, himself a transgender man, writes:

> It is difficult, if not impossible, for most cisgender therapists to comprehend the degree and intensity of these feelings for transgender adolescents. When young transgender boys look in the mirror and see breasts developing, their gender dysphoria shoots through the roof. It becomes impossible to go to school in the morning because none of their shirts fit right. No matter what they do, those breasts are visible to others. This is why transgender boys bind their chests—with binders made for this purpose if they can afford them, if not, they use ACE bandages or duct tape. The horror of beginning to menstruate is almost unimaginable.[22]

We experienced both the issues Nealy highlights. One struggling teenager we cared for used duct tape to bind their breasts. Of course, one doesn't go into the bathroom with a teenager so we never saw the binding. However, we saw the large quantities of discarded duct tape in the bedroom trash can. We were really naive at this point in our fostering journey. We were unaware of what the tape was being used for. Jane enquired why there was so much tape in the trash and learnt about breast binding.

In addition, Jane found blood-stained boxers hidden in the under-the-eaves storage where we keep Christmas decorations and suitcases. It all added up to a young person who was confused and embarrassed by their body. Facial hair and other biological signs of masculinity appearing at puberty will lead to the same confusion in a trans girl.

Other teenagers may still be questioning their gender identity. Lizzie had just turned thirteen when she and her younger brother were placed with us. After a few months, Lizzie told us that she was unsure about gender and wanted to start living as a boy. At the beginning, Lizzie told us she only wanted to explore boys' clothes and was keeping her name. She had her long hair cut short. Then she sorted out all her clothing, keeping only gender-neutral garments. Some new clothes and underwear were purchased. Soon afterwards Lizzie decided to explore a new name, and chose to use "he" as a pronoun. Hunter was to be the new name. A few months later Hunter told us he was still uncertain about gender and wanted to go back to living as a girl with the next set of new clothes. Again, another few months later, Lizzie once again explored living as a boy. It was at this point Hunter left our care. We don't want to give the impression that each exploration was just a quick announcement, followed by a change of gender. Each entailed much conversation with us, together with all the consideration about what it would mean with school and peers. We have kept in touch. Hunter is now living as Lizzie, but we suspect is still questioning gender identity.

As empathic re-parents the only thing we could offer was complete acceptance as these adolescents were transitioning and questioning. We did not question their choice of clothes, happily buying boxer shorts and male clothing as chosen. We had long talks about their decisions including trying out different names as a name appropriate to their gender was being selected.

This was many years ago and we wish we had the understanding then that we have now. We would have been better able to advocate for these young people in school and provide more substantive help. However, we do hope knowing they were accepted without reservation was what these young people needed. Nealy comments, "We want our identity to be acknowledged and validated by those around us—particularly by those who are important to us, the people we love and who love us, our family."[23]

Our desire is that future carers will be better equipped to be empathic re-parents to transgender youth. The Williams Institute recently showed that 150,000 youth (aged 13–17) identify as transgender. This is 0.7 percent of the population in that age range.[24] In 2011, the National Center of Transgender Equality carried out a study that revealed for these adolescents 82 percent felt unsafe at school; 44 percent had been physically abused; 67 percent had been bullied online and 64 percent had their property stolen or destroyed.[25] In other words, transgender youth are in greater danger of violence, and hence of trauma induced by that violence, than other youth.

Nealy adds, "For these transgender adolescents, the risk of depression, hopelessness and suicide are acute."[26] Teenagers in foster care are already at a high risk of these due to their traumatic past resulting in higher ACE scores. As empathic re-parents we want to reduce the trauma for the kids in our care and help them heal from past trauma. Therefore, it is essential that their gender issues are handled in the best way possible.

The teenagers we have fostered who have identified as gay or lesbian have not seemed to experience the same problems as those who were transgender. Perhaps that is because we live in a city that prides itself on being gay-friendly, and our schools and community are generally accepting of LGBTQ+. Even so, it's important to emphasize empathic carers need to be comfortable with people identifying as gay so they can be genuinely accepting of all the young people in their home.

Bodies Do Matter

Another area that requires careful empathic re-parenting is with body image. Many teenagers who have come into our care have suffered from an eating disorder. We talked briefly about this in *Welcoming Strangers*.

Many are overweight, often unhealthily so. We have been asked by their pediatricians to help them lose weight, especially when they are already showing signs that the weight is harming them (through elevated levels in blood tests, asthma and stress on joints). This adds an additional dilemma: how do we help this child lose weight without making them feel embarrassed or ashamed about their bodies? Many of them are already feeling in despair having been the recipients of teasing and bullying from peers because of their weight. Their self-image is terrible. We don't want to add to their poor self-image by telling them they need to diet!

One of the first things we can do is make sure that their clothing is appropriate for their age. This can be quite time-consuming, especially with teenage girls. Many of the larger sizes are more geared at an older age group, which is always a source of frustration. However, it can be done and it is very important that these young people feel good about themselves. It is worth the time and effort to send a child to school feeling they look good and knowing they will fit in with peers.

*

"I want skinny jeans. You know, those really tight ones," demanded Dean. "Everyone in my class is wearing them. I really need some."

Dean had been living with us for a couple of weeks. We were on a shopping expedition to buy him some much-needed clothes. Dean was eleven, a little heavier than most of his classmates, and clearly anxious to fit in with his peers. Finding skinny jeans in Dean's size was not going to be easy! We scoured the various stores eventually managing to find some that fit him, but they were about eighteen inches too long. Dean didn't care. He was delighted with them. A little bit of snipping and hemming helped with the length. Dean had skinny jeans and he felt good about himself.

*

Nevaeh was also eleven. She was medically obese and it was already significantly affecting her health. She wasn't very tall for her age but needed XL adult sizes in clothing. Nevaeh was still very much a little girl. In addition to playing with her toys she loved to watch children's programs on television. Her favorites included *SpongeBob SquarePants* and *Dora the Explorer*. She wanted nothing more than to wear clothing depicting these characters. It was hard to find appropriate clothing for her. We found that by buying capris in the adult sizes they fitted her perfectly as jeans or more formal pants. Again, we scoured various stores looking for sweaters and shirts that either depicted characters from various shows or that look more childlike. Eventually we managed to put together a wardrobe suitable for a young eleven-year-old. She was delighted, especially as her teachers and peers all told her how wonderful she looked.

*

The National Center for Biotechnology Information (NCBI) published a report in 2015 about weight and body image perceptions.[27] The paper collates and discusses information from many studies on body image, most of which have been written since the 1980s. The perception of body image and the resulting dissatisfaction in how one looks plays a large part in teenagers developing eating disorders. Adolescents who have suffered trauma are at an even greater risk, teenagers in foster care would definitely fall into this category.

The original impetus for the ACE study came when Dr. Vincent Felitti ran a clinic at Kaiser Permanente for people struggling with obesity. He noticed that the drop-out rate was at 50 percent despite people being successful in the program. He conducted interviews with the 286 people who had left the program.[28] Felitti discovered that the majority had been victims of childhood sexual abuse. He was surprised and concerned by his findings. In 1990, he presented his research to the North American Association for the Study of Obesity at Atlanta. It was not initially well received, but it was at that meeting he met Dr. Anda from the CDC and together they went on to formulate the ACE study.

In addition to the increased propensity for eating disorders due to their history of trauma teenagers in foster care share all the same risks as any other adolescent. The report from the NCBI notes that "the greatest decline in body satisfaction occurred in girls under the age of 19 following exposure to overtly thin media images."[29] Peer pressure is a huge influence, especially where teenagers are isolated and judged according to weight. In addition, it was reported that "Body dissatisfaction among tenth grade girls was strongly predicted by the belief that thinness was critical to their attraction to boys."[30]

It is not just criticism from peers that is a concern. The paper from the NCBI also notes, "Research has shown that weight-based teasing from parents and siblings is associated with body dissatisfaction among girls and drive for muscularity among boys in eighth and ninth grade."

All the negative body image and dissatisfaction can lead to eating disorders (anorexia, bulimia, binge eating disorder). We have experienced children in foster care who are already trapped in an eating disorder spiral. Though we have never had a teenager with an eating disorder that was severe enough to require hospitalization, we have had several teens who have caused us some anxiety, and at times needed us to seek professional help for them. Eating disorders are an area that can leave foster carers feeling very vulnerable, especially with the anorexic teen who won't eat anything or hearing a teen rush to the bathroom to vomit after eating a hearty meal. Eating disorders are often accompanied by denial from teenagers, with the ensuing refusal to talk about it:

"I do eat loads, you just don't see me."

"I had lots to eat at school today. I'm too full to eat."

"I wasn't throwing up. You must have heard someone else."

These are often accompanied by self-loathing comments:

"I'm too fat."

"Look how my stomach sticks out."

"Nobody likes you if you are fat."

*

One teenage girl we cared for whose eating disorder caused her to vomit after a meal hated her body. She was stereotypically attractive: petite, blonde and blue-eyed. She would only make friends with girls who were heavier than she was. She was quite open and vocal about it. She only wanted, in her words, "fat friends"—although none of her friends could ever have been described as overweight—so that she would always look like the skinny one and therefore the prettiest.

Often our only recourse is to keep affirming each teenager as valuable, and trying to help them feel good about themselves.

Eating disorders don't just affect teenagers, although they are more commonly seen in that age group. Younger children too often have at least the seeds of eating disorders. The violence and trauma experienced have resulted in them feeling worthless, and with no control over their lives. This can even happen before the children are old enough to verbalize these feelings.

*

Ava was only three when she and her twelve-month-old baby brother came to live with us, and stayed for about a year. Ultimately, they went to separate adoptive homes (never a decision taken lightly) as that would ensure they received the individual care they needed. When they arrived they were timid and withdrawn. Ava had very little speech, while her brother was barely able to crawl. They did not look well cared for, but neither of the children looked underweight. They proved to be very good eaters, and ate well refusing nothing prepared for them, which is always nice to see. Then came the shock; after most meals Ava made herself vomit. Sometimes she used her fingers, and sometimes she seemed to be able to regurgitate at will. Medical reasons were quickly eliminated. Although with careful non-violent re-parenting the situation improved, even after she left us she would continue to need help, which her adoptive parents were willing to provide.

Her little brother screamed. And what a scream! It was high pitched, very loud and lasted for several minutes. Every time a meal or his bottle ended he screamed. We are aware that not being fed regularly can produce an inner panic when food ends. Nevertheless, the trauma of his first few months was manifesting itself as an eating problem. As he grew and started to toddle we had to be increasingly diligent, as any liquid or anything resembling food would be ingested. On one occasion when he toddled up to the table just before dinner, he reached up and grabbed the vinegar. He tipped his head back and gulped down half the bottle before Jane crossed the room to take it. That resulted in a quick visit to the emergency doctor who assured us that no harm had been done.

*

Tiana, too, had a problem with binge eating. She did not make herself regurgitate as Ava did, but would eat and eat until her body could not hold anymore. Then she would vomit. After each time she vomited, she would ask could she have more food as now she had room. If she saw food, she simply had to eat it all. It was irresistible for her.

We had learned, toward the beginning of the placement, that taking Tiana to an all-you-can-eat buffet was a disaster. After she had been with us a few weeks we went out to our local Indian buffet. It is a favorite restaurant of the family, and we often visit for Sunday lunch. We had already taken Tiana out to eat in restaurants, and she had really enjoyed the experience. However, we had not visited the buffet. It was a disaster. We realized that

Tiana had problems with food, but felt that we would be able to help her serve herself. We knew she would want to visit the buffet twice, so planned appropriately helping her take a first plateful of moderate size. After she had eaten it, before we could even tell her we would take her for a second helping, she was up and reached the buffet. It was so fast! She had already heaped her plate before we could reach her. As she continued to eat we could see that she was so full she was really struggling. She was even talking about how she would finish quickly so she could go back for more food. We tried to explain to her that buffets were not meant for people to eat everything, but to give a choice. Tiana spent the afternoon throwing up! Yet it made no impression on her. We decided it was probably a good idea not to do buffets with Tiana for the foreseeable future.

We also needed to be careful about what snacks were purchased when Tiana lived with us. We could no longer keep snacks in the kitchen cupboard on a help yourself basis. They had to be put away, limited to being given to all the children when they got home from school (the usual time the snack supply was raided!). Tiana continued to have problems related to food all the time she was with us. Sadly, she still does, although now in her mid-teens at the time of writing. She is no longer a member of our household, but we have frequent phone chats. Each time she phones she begins the conversation by talking about what she has eaten that day, and tries to assure us that she is trying to lose weight. Our tactic is usually to say something benign, and change the subject giving her lots of praise for things she has done well at school or in the community.

*

Tiana and Ava's stories serve to illustrate the damage that has been done even to young children, the effects of which continue for many years. Eating disorders have long term effects both physically and psychologically. As empathic re-parents we have to ensure that we try to understand a little of what the young person is thinking and feeling. Dealing with teenagers and children with eating disorders can be an emotional roller-coaster ride for any re-parent.

There is a further complexity when, as in the case of Nevaeh (above), the eating disorder led to an eleven-year-old who was having serious health issues. Her pediatrician advised us to help her lose weight as quickly, and safely, as possible. As noted above this dilemma for the re-parent is always a hard one. We needed to help Nevaeh lose weight without giving any negative implications about her size, and how she looked, or making her feel food deprived. It can be quite difficult! We have faced it with several children. Each child is different so there is no one correct way, and we probably made lots of mistakes along the way.

With Nevaeh, as with Tiana, we noticed that she always liked to have a second helping, and felt stressed if that was denied. We planned her portion sizes so that she always got her "seconds." She always wanted to have dessert after a meal, so we bought bite-sized chocolate bars and she could choose one as her dessert. We implemented a limit on drinks with high calorific value. We simply had two lists of drinks. One list she could have as many drinks as she liked, whenever she wanted to. The other side of her list she could pick two a day and choose when she had them.

Her school had noticed that she would eat any food others in her class left from their breakfasts and lunches. They were very supportive and implemented a no sharing food rule. They also made sure Nevaeh had healthy snacks at school. We emphasized that we did not want her to feel different, and stressed that she should always be included in any class celebrations and have a piece of birthday cake or cupcake whenever the other children did. It worked well for Nevaeh, she lost weight slowly and appropriately with monthly check-ins at the doctor to monitor progress. At the same time as being deliberate about what she ate, without mentioning the word diet, we encouraged her to be more active than she had in the past. She especially enjoyed learning to swim and walking the dogs with us.

*

Our above stories demonstrate how to be an empathic re-parent, to counteract the violence children have suffered through race and gender issues. As well as becoming empathic ourselves, we want to help the children develop empathy for others. When we took our first set of siblings near to the beginning of our foster care journey we made several assumptions. One of these was that if the children came from a family where the adults were abusive then they would of necessity be very close. Another was that being put into a home with strangers a sibling group would bond together. Nothing was further from the truth. The kids often simply ignored each other. Each was locked in their own little world and they did not care what happened to the other. There was no empathy for each other, no compassion if one was hurting, and often no attempt to comfort each other. Teenagers and older children would even vocalize that they hated each other, and wished that their siblings had been placed with a different family. We also saw physical aggression toward each other, which we were quick to stop, reminding the kids that we were a nonviolent household.

This lack of empathy and disregard for each other came as an initial surprise to us. We quickly realized that when a child has never bonded with a parent they were unable to bond with a sibling. At the time of writing the latest research on attachment and bonding has confirmed our observations. Bruce Perry, who leads the Child Trauma Institute, comments:

> One of the major problems with these [maltreated] children is aggression and cruelty. This is related to two primary problems in neglected children: (1) lack of empathy and (2) poor impulse control. The ability to emotionally "understand" the impact of your behavior on others is impaired in these children. They really do not understand or feel what

it is like for others when they do or say something hurtful. Indeed, these children often feel compelled to lash out and hurt others—most typically something less powerful than they are. They will hurt animals, smaller children, peers and siblings. One of the most disturbing elements of this aggression is that it is often accompanied by a detached, cold lack of empathy. They may show regret (an intellectual response) but not remorse (an emotional response) when confronted about their aggressive or cruel behaviors.[31]

In all our years fostering, we only had one set of siblings—two half-sisters, aged eleven and thirteen—who were bonded. These two were very close and did lots of things together. All the others showed the traits described above. However, it is important that siblings are kept together wherever possible. Not only is it desirable, but the law demands it. A clause in the Fostering Connections to Success and Increasing Adoptions Act of 2008 (H.R. 6893) reads:

> (Sec. 206) Requires a state plan to provide for reasonable efforts for joint placement of siblings in the same foster care, kinship guardianship, or adoptive placement unless it would be contrary to the safety or well-being of any of them. Requires the plan also to provide, in the case of siblings removed from their homes who are not jointly placed, for frequent visitation or other ongoing interaction between the siblings, unless it would be contrary to the safety or well-being of any of them.[32]

About two-thirds of children in foster care have a sibling also in foster care.[33] Research shows that placing siblings together is ultimately always advantageous for their well-being.[34] Therefore, it is an important part of re-parenting to help the children and teenagers develop an empathic relationship with their siblings.

Sibling relationships are important for their future. We have both maintained strong ties with our own siblings, although physically we are far apart. The strength of our relationships has kept us in close contact. On the occasions when we meet up it feels like we have not been apart, and we easily chat and enjoy time together. We see the same thing in our three birth children who are all adults now and physically distant from each other. We want to teach siblings to have empathy for each other, thus beginning the process of a healthy relationship with each other. Or perhaps more accurately, we should say we want to begin the process of teaching brothers and sisters to have empathy toward each other.

This can be really hard when faced with young people who can barely be left safely in the same room due to their aggression—both physically and with hurtful words. It takes much time, patience and commitment on the part of re-parents. Nor is it just applicable to sibling relationships. We have found that many children who have been victims of violence show little empathy towards animals. We have welcomed children to our home who will try to hurt our pugs. One child tried to hit them with a metal bar when she was feeling angry. Another would threaten to kill them. We had to be careful always to monitor children around pets.

Nor do they have empathy with the plight of other human beings. They don't care if others are hurting and will express that. We have had children who mock those with disabilities, even when living in the same household. We remember having two teenage girls when we welcomed a third boy. He was only going to be with us for three weeks as he was awaiting placement in a specialized residential facility. The developmental delays were more severe than we had anticipated. These included him needing constant watching as he was apt to wander off and get lost (it was this trait that had necessitated the need for a facility that could provide round-the-clock care). The two girls were merciless in their teasing, which bordered on being cruel, although they thought they were being funny. We had to have numerous conversations with them about kindness and empathy.

Similar reactions ensued with many teenagers when seeing the plight of others on television news and media sites. The tendency is to laugh and mock, rather than be unsettled by the images. Not that we think that kids being bombarded by repeated coverage of tragedies by the media is a good thing for them, but how unmoved they are does illustrate the lack of empathy their personal experience of violence has caused.

Final Things We Have Learned

How are we to find empathy and care for children placed with us whose life and cultural experiences we have not shared? And in turn, how are we to help children develop empathy toward other people?

1.

We faced our own inner prejudices. It's likely that most of us feel that we are not prejudiced. How often have you heard, "I'm not prejudiced, but . . ."? Because there is social disapproval of prejudice, to admit to being prejudiced would be to acknowledge some moral failing.

However, it is impossible not to be prejudiced, for prejudice is an assumption, a prejudgment, and prejudgments are simply the way we make sense of things. We prejudge that things will be just the way they were yesterday—that the floor will still take our weight when we get out of bed, that water will flow from the faucet, that our loved ones will still relate to us in meaningful ways. Our experiences allow us to form assumptions to help us navigate through life. But, not all assumptions are warranted. Jane does not like to fly. She enters the airport with an assumption that something bad might happen. No matter how many times Andy presents evidence that air travel is far safer than driving a car, Jane holds a prejudice about flying.

And she's not alone. Yet, based on the evidence, a bias against air transport is unwarranted.

Other prejudices are more harmful, especially assumptions we do not know we have. German philosopher Hans-Georg Gadamer warned about the "tyranny of hidden prejudice." If our prejudgments are obvious, we can more easily deal with unwarranted ones. However, if our prejudice is hidden, it can have an unhelpful affect. Usually, hidden prejudices remain hidden until we face a situation that challenges the prejudice.

*

The optometrist had a deal. Buy two pairs of glasses for the price of one; make one pair prescription sunglasses. Always ready for a deal, Andy ordered his new glasses—tinted deep red. On a first outing with the family, driving down an English motorway, Andy repeatedly commented at the vibrant colors of the flowers along the roadside. The kids in the back exchanged looks.

"Mum, is everything OK with dad?"

Oblivious, Andy continued to comment on the depth of the reds along the motorway.

It gradually dawned on him. He was literally seeing through "rose-tinted spectacles." Everything he saw was colored by his prescription sunglasses, and the insipid pinks picked up a new and deeper brilliance. Our prejudices are often unknown to us, as we view the world through the lenses of our socialization, education and worldview.

2.

We accepted the children as they were, and became supportive of their struggles. When we began foster care in the early 1980s, ourselves only just in our adulthood, we both had a fairly conventional view of gender, and our prejudices about race, culture, and ethnicity were largely buried under an assumed "white as normative" view of the world. It has often been the children we have cared for who have challenged our assumptions about life. It was accepting our children as they were, without trying to impose our assumptions about what they ought to be, that brought greater openness and change within ourselves.

3.

We developed empathic awareness by trying to think of situations we had been in that had been strange to us. These we talked about together and recalled how we felt. Choosing to live in a different culture has largely been this way for us. Almost every time we speak in the presence of strangers, we are asked, "Where are you from?" We have learned, perhaps cheekily, to answer with our home town in the U.S.A. Our interlocutors often look puzzled, and most times we spare their embarrassment by explaining that we came from the U.K. After 23 years it wears a little thin, but is a more or less constant reminder what it must feel like to be different because of skin color, or gender preference, or because we do not fit within our gender assigned at birth. Of course, we can never know those feelings, but our difference gives us at least a hint.

4.

We helped children become empathic themselves. We try to help them to feel a little of what the other feels. It is a long, slow process which needs to be done frequently and consistently on the part of the re-parent. Generally we try to reframe any sentences that could start "don't do that . . ." in a way designed to show empathy:

> "Poor doggie, you'll hurt her if you kick her."

> "Your sister feels really bad that you called her that name, look you made her cry."

> "Look at those poor people on the television, they are really hungry."

Trying to help the children be involved in some kind of charity work also helps the process of teaching the children to be empathic. Most of our teenagers have been involved with The Learning Web.[35] In our area, there is a wonderful worker designated to provide teenagers in foster care with life skills. As well as the more readily recognized life skills—cookery classes, how to use a launderette, banking, riding the public bus system—she included many activities which would help develop empathy. Our teenagers went to the SPCA to care for the animals, they helped to prepare and serve meals through a local organization to feed those who were homeless or hungry, and they went to nursing homes to give manicures, play games and sing.

5.

We realized that many things were outside our own life experiences so reached out for help when out of our depth. To be a racial minority was outside of our experience. So, too, was to be differently gendered, or to have an eating disorder. Realizing our inadequacies, we reached out to others. We have black friends and coworkers to whom we talked. We asked our friends and family in the LGBTQ+ community for insight. We listened and tried to understand.

6.

We became allies and advocates. By philosophical commitment, we are pluralists. We have grown to love the diversity of the world with all its cultures, ideas, customs, religions, and ways of being and doing things. Pluralism moves beyond mere toleration of difference (though that is a good place to start) and into a celebration of our differences as we learn from all. Letting our kids realize that we weren't just tolerating things but celebrated with them the difference they brought to our family has been a great help. In such a loving, supportive and intentionally nonviolent home we hope we have helped them experience healing of their trauma—at least a little.

Notes

1 Abraham Lincoln, *First Inaugural Address* (New Haven, CT: Yale Law School, Avalon Project in Law History and Diplomacy, n.d.), 7.
2 For the most comprehensive statistical analysis of those killed see the work of Matthew White at http://necrometrics.com/index.htm, and his book *Atrocities: The 100 Deadliest Episodes in Human History* (New York: W. W. Norton, 2012).
3 Steven Pinker, *The Better Angels of Our Nature: Why Violence Has Declined* (New York: Viking, 2011).
4 White, *Atrocities*, 541.
5 Pinker, *Better Angels*, 573.
6 Rae Greiner, "1909: The Introduction of the Word 'Empathy' into English," in *BRANCH: Britain, Representation and Nineteenth-Century History*, edited by Dino Franco Felluga (Extension of Romanticism and Victorianism on the Net, 2018), 2.
7 René Descartes, *Discourse on Method and Meditations on First Philosophy*, Trans. Donald A. Cress. (Indianapolis, IN: Hackett, 1998), 32.
8 Peter Singer, *Animal Liberation* (New York: Harper Perennial, 2009), 6.
9 Frans de Waal, *The Age of Empathy: Nature's Lessons for a Kinder Society* (New York: Three Rivers Press, 2009), 43.
10 Jeremy Rifkin, *The Empathic Civilization: The Race to Global Consciousness in a World of Crisis*, (New York: Jeremy P. Tarcher/Penguin, 2009), 1.
11 Ibid., 10.
12 Ibid., 66–81.
13 Ibid., 43.
14 City-Data, "Ithaca NY," www.city-data.com/city/Ithaca-New-York.html, accessed February 22, 2018.
15 Gregory A. Kompes, *50 Fabulous Gay-Friendly Places to Live* (Franklin Lakes, NJ: Career Press, 2005).
16 Karen E. Fields and Barbara J. Fields, *Racecraft: The Soul of Inequality in American Life* (New York: Versa, 2012), 2.
17 See Pinker, *Better Angels*, 382–385.
18 Chart in ibid., 386, and latest data, U.S. Department of Justice, Federal Bureau of Investigation, Criminal Justice Information Services Division, "2016 Hate Crime Statistics," https://ucr.fbi.gov/hate-crime/2016/tables/table-2, accessed March 14, 2018.
19 Adam Rutherford, "Why Racism is Not Backed by Science," *The Observer*, March 1, 2015, www.theguardian.com/science/2015/mar/01/racism-science-human-genomes-darwin. accessed March 14, 2018.
20 Peter L. Berger and Thomas Luckmann, *The Social Construction of Reality: A Treatise in the Sociology of Knowledge* (New York: Anchor, 1967).
21 Andrew Fitz-Gibbon, "Today I Am Black Too, or Why Racism is Unsustainable," *The Abbot's Blog*, June 21, 2015, https://lindisfarnecommunity.blogspot.com/2015/06/today-i-black-too-or-why-racism-is.html.

22 Elijah C. Nealy, *Transgender Children and Youth: Cultivating Pride and Joy with Families in Transition* (New York: W. W. Norton, 2017), 118.
23 Ibid., xv.
24 The Williams Institute, "New Estimates Show that 150,000 Youth Ages 13 to 17 Identify as Transgender," UCLA School of Law, January 17, 2017, https://williamsinstitute.law.ucla.edu/research/transgender-issues/new-estimates-show-that-150000-youth-ages-13-to-17-identify-as-transgender-in-the-us, accessed March 1, 2018.
25 No Bullying, "Transgender Bullying: A National Epidemic," December 22, 2015, https://nobullying.com/transgender-bullying, accessed March 1, 2018.
26 Nealy, *Transgender Children and Youth*, xvii.
27 Dana K. Voelker, Justine J. Reed and Christy Greenleaf, "Weight Status and Body Image in Adolescents: Current Perspectives," National Center for Biotechnology Information, August 25, 2015, www.ncbi.nlm.nih.gov/pmc/articles/PMC4554432, accessed March 14, 2018.
28 Jane Ellen Stevens, "Toxic Stress from Childhood Trauma Causes Obesity, Too," May 23, 2012, https://acestoohigh.com/2012/05/23/toxic-stress-from-childhood-trauma-causes-obesity-too, accessed March 14, 2018.
29 Ibid.
30 Ibid.
31 Bruce D. Perry, "Bonding and Attachment in Maltreated Children: Consequences of Emotional Neglect in Childhood," 2018, http://teacher.scholastic.com/professional/bruceperry/bonding.htm, accessed March 30, 2018 (adapted in part from *Maltreated Children: Experience, Brain Development and the Next Generation*, New York: W. W. Norton & Company, in preparation).
32 Congress.gov, "Fostering Connections to Success and Increasing Adoptions Act of 2008," www.congress.gov/bill/110th-congress/house-bill/6893, accessed April 2, 2008.
33 Child Welfare Information Gateway, "Sibling Issues in Foster Care," January 2013, www.childwelfare.gov/pubpdfs/siblingissues.pdf, accessed April 2, 2018.
34 Ibid.
35 See www.learning-web.org.

3 Nurturing Our Better Angel of Self-Control

Over the years, we have held many conversations with children in our care with regard to technology. The dawn of the internet age, followed by the smart phone caused a whole lot of new issues for foster parents. Suddenly, teens and younger children had a whole new world opened to them. We have loved the rise in technology, and are both ardent Apple users. We were not first adopters, but pretty close to the beginning. Macs were simply too expensive. We bought our first Macintosh LC in 1990, and first laptop, the Powerbook 100, in 1992. LC stood for "low cost," but at over $4,000 in 2018 terms, it was still quite a financial stretch. Since then we have been shamelessly hooked. Everything we have ever written has been on Macs, and during our writing periods you will find us side by side, tapping away on our Macbooks. One of the better aspects of technology has been our ability to keep in touch with family and friends through social media. Both of us have re-connected with distant relatives and old school friends through Facebook. "Facetiming" our grandchildren, anytime, anywhere from our phones, has been a delight. We wish our children could have kept in touch with their grandparents in the same way when they were growing up. We are both committed to foster children having access to age-appropriate technology to ensure their experiences are the same as their peers. Yet, we can't ignore the new dimension it has brought to foster care, certainly not making the task of re-parenting the teen any easier. Our kids and their friends have instant communication. This can be good, but has its disadvantages too.

Jack wanted to stay out to midnight. We had said no. As with many families, we do sometimes allow kids to stay out late, but this is reserved for special occasions with all the usual provisos of where they will be, who they will be with, and how they will get home. Jack knew that we wouldn't agree before he asked, and wasn't greatly upset. In fact, we think he would have been shocked if we had said yes, and he wouldn't have had anything to do anyway. Regardless, he got on Facebook saying, "My foster parents are mean." Immediately, lots of kids responded giving him sympathy and wild advice on how to run away and leave home. Jack knew we would have seen his post, as Jane was his Facebook friend. He seemed to think it was all a bit of a joke. Even so, if he had been really upset it could have made him angry and resentful, and made the incident into something much bigger than it was.

*

Lisa was thirteen. She was placed with us because of truancy. No matter how hard her parents and various workers had tried to encourage her, she had refused to go to school. They had no control over Lisa. So, through the court system she was placed in foster care.

We realized quickly that part of the problem was her "addiction" to her electronics. With computer, tablet, and phones, she came well equipped! The problem was she couldn't put them away. It didn't matter whether it was video games, social media on phones, or movies on any available device, so long as it was on one of her many screens Lisa was glued to it. She had no ability to self-regulate.

It was this "addiction" to electronics that was a big contributing factor to her truancy. She would play games until she dropped asleep exhausted in the early hours of the morning. Then after a couple of hours sleep she was awoken to get up to go to school. At home, she had simply refused. Living with us she went to school, but in her first couple of weeks Jane had several phone calls from school saying she was very tired, and she had gone to the nurse's office to sleep.

We tried talking to her. Lisa was quiet and well behaved in the home, and was pleasant and polite to us. We had tried to explain the need for enough sleep as part of keeping herself healthy and doing well at school. She always agreed that was what she wanted to do. Ultimately, she wanted to get back home, and that was certainly our and the agency's aim. Yet, the pull of technology proved too strong.

We decided, as Lisa had no internal regulation, that we would have to help by providing an external control. We talked with the caseworker and suggested that Lisa be required to leave all her electronics downstairs at her bedtime. We assured Lisa we had no interest in looking at her phone or tablet and we did not want to know the passwords. She could leave them on their chargers in a place of her choosing. We would not touch them. She agreed to the plan. She even seemed quite happy with it.

Quickly, the daytime tiredness ceased to be a problem. Her attendance was excellent and her grades started to improve. The school was pleased with her. Then came her birthday and a long weekend at home. She had a lovely time and we hoped this would be a big step forward in the plan for her future return home.

She came back quite excitedly. "Look, Jane and Andy," she called as soon as she was out of her father's car. "Dad bought me a new phone for my birthday. Look at all the things it does!"

Even though her parents were both out of work they had bought Lisa an expensive piece of hardware. We admired her latest acquisition, and listened to her tales of her weekend home. When it was bedtime Lisa plugged her computer, tablet, and the phone into their respective chargers for their overnight sojourn.

"Lisa, what about your old phone?" Jane asked. "That needs to come down, too."

"Oh, I left that at my mom's house," replied Lisa.

"Are you sure?" Jane pushed, "We don't want any electronics upstairs."

"No, I haven't got anything, I promise," she said very innocently.

A couple of weeks later we were having our usual before-kids-get-up spell in the hot tub.

Jane broached the subject: "I'm a bit worried about Lisa. Something is not quite right. I had another email from the school yesterday. She is not getting her work done, they think she seems a bit tired."

"Hmmm," replied Andy, "We'll have to keep an eye on that. Do you think she has got another phone or tablet hidden upstairs?"

"Well, I have wondered that," mused Jane. "But I can't very well search her room." (We have never searched teenagers' rooms as we want to build trust.)

The nagging worry remained in our minds as we moved on to other topics. A week later a school progress report showed that Lisa's grades were slipping, although she was still passing all her subjects. We re-visited the discussion.

"I definitely think Lisa has something she is playing with at night," Jane said.

"Anything you are seeing besides the falling grades?" Andy responded.

"Well yes," Jane replied. "This probably seems silly but I have been noticing that she goes to the bathroom a couple of hours after bedtime every night."

Our bedroom and bathroom are on the first floor. The rest of the bedrooms and children's bathroom are upstairs. We often hear the patter of feet walking down the hallway to the bathroom, which is above our heads!

"Oh, that doesn't sound silly at all." Andy commented, "That would just be the timing of a movie, and I know she had some downloaded on her old phone. What do you think we should do?"

"Well, she is going home for the weekend. When she comes back we can ask her if she has any additional electronics. That will give us the opportunity to reiterate that she cannot have them in her room at night."

"Good plan! It will also give her a chance to be truthful and admit she has got something without being embarrassed that she lied to us."

The weekend passed without incident. As usual, Lisa had a great time on her visit home. On return we asked if she had enjoyed herself, and she told us what she had done. When bedtime came we reminded her that if she had brought any more electronics they too had to be placed on chargers at night. She looked us straight in the eye and assured us she had no more with her. She looked so innocent we almost wondered if our suspicions had been wrong. But we had gained a lot of experience of teenagers by that time!

A couple of days later we were ready to go to bed, but Lisa still hadn't brought her electronics down. Lisa had always been very good at respecting the time she was required to place them on the chargers, so it was unusual for her to be late.

Jane called up the stairs, "Lisa, can you bring your stuff down? We are ready to go to bed, and I want to put all the lights off."

"I'm in the shower," came the muffled voice.

"Okay, I'll just grab them off your desk. I'll put them on their chargers for you," Jane replied.

Jane went into Lisa's room to get the laptop, tablet, and phone. Unfortunately, or maybe fortunately, the phone was plugged into the wall on a dual charger. The second wire went under Lisa's pillow and was attached to a second phone! Our suspicions had been correct. A very quick conversation ensued where we told Lisa that lying and deceiving were not ways to gain trust. Then it was really bedtime for all of us!

Our style is that when something has happened in the household we address it but we don't keep endlessly revisiting it, and once a subject has been addressed we move on. However, a couple of sentences spoken late at night did not really feel sufficient to address the multiple lies we had been told. It needed further discussion. So, after school the next day we broached the subject. We didn't make it a long discussion. No arguments, no raised voices, Jane just reiterated that it was disappointing that she had lied about the second phone. We did not receive any apologies, or see any remorse. Lisa told us that she only used it for an alarm, and not for anything else. As Jane woke her, and the other teens in the household, each day she knew that no alarm had gone off on any morning. However, the nocturnal visits to the bathroom ceased. If it had truly only been needed for an alarm the secrecy was equally disturbing. During the discussion, Lisa even asked if we could change the rule and trust her as she had gone to school every day! Of course, we said that we wanted her to keep on leaving all the electronics on charge as that was, in part, helping her be successful.

This same scenario was repeated twice more in the couple of years Lisa was with us. We could not get her to show much interest in anything that wasn't technology. She didn't want to join the family on a camping vacation, or even day trips. She was offered a great work experience placement in a job she chose. Unfortunately, she was not able to sustain working as it took away time from her Xbox. Ironically the work placement would have given her more money to purchase more technology! Anything that took her away from her gadgets was unwelcomed.

Even though Lisa was doing reasonably well at school we still got phone calls and emails from her high school on many occasions asking if we could talk to her about using the phone or iPad during lessons. Often it was discovered under a text book or on her knee under the desk. Her school was generous in allowing students to use their phones during breaks. Lisa was supposed to restrict her usage to those times. Even so, regardless of how many times we had that conversation within a few days the same problem occurred. In the moment, while she was talking to us she seemed sincere. Lisa's intentions may have been good, yet we knew she had not learned enough self-control to have the ego-strength to overcome the urge to get on the electronics if they were in the same room as her. Ultimately, her inability to control her technology use worked against her best interests. Yet, with time and care Lisa did begin to develop inner regulation and she was able to return home.

*

In large part, Lisa's "addiction" problems—we'll come back below to be more specific about addiction—were rooted in a lack of self-control. She just couldn't help herself. But where did this inability to moderate her own behavior come from? There is a growing body of evidence to suggest that, according to award-winning journalist Maia Szalavitz, who covers addiction issues for *The New York Times*, *Time Magazine*, and *Scientific American*, "for many, if not all people with addiction, trauma is perhaps *the* critical factor that causes the problem."[1] From her work in countless interviews with people with various addictions she found substantial correlation between, for example, women who abused substances with a history of rape, or bullying, or physical and emotional abuse in their childhoods. She says:

> At least two thirds of addicted people have suffered at least one extremely traumatic experience during childhood—and the higher the exposure to trauma, the greater the addiction risk . . . Further, the more extreme the addiction, generally, the more extreme the childhood history of trauma.[2]

Tellingly, Szalavitz suggests that:

> If you learn the world is not a safe and stable place—and that others are unreliable—when you are young, it can shape the trajectory of your emotional learning and the way you cope with the rest of your life.[3]

Might it be that Lisa's exposure to violence in her early years, and the subsequent trauma she suffered, was in part a contributory factor in her inability to exercise self-control with regard to behaviors that were ultimately not in her best interests? It seems likely. We saw in Chapter 1 that the higher the ACE score (adverse childhood experiences) the greater likelihood of difficulties later in life. Van de Kolk argues that such experiences and their accompanying trauma are best overcome in a safe and loving environment. Our suggestion is, that when children in our care exhibit lack of self-control, and possibly addiction, that loving nonviolent re-parenting provides just such a safe space, not only to heal from their trauma, but also to develop those aspects of normal psychological development that they have missed—in this instance, the better angel of self-control.

So far as we can tell, philosophers have from the beginning struggled with the notion that human nature is difficult to control. It is the human lot to wrestle with an unruly inner life. We do things we don't want to do. We do things we ought not to. Even those things we would really like to do we can't find a way to do them. We eat too much, or eat the wrong things, but feel powerless to do anything other. We know we ought to bite our tongue, but instead say things we wish we hadn't. Impulses seem too often to be like an unruly animal that we can't control. It's all the more of concern when those unruly impulses are violent ones—the man who cannot control his urge to beat his partner, the mother who is seemingly unable to control lashing out at the kids with a hairbrush, shoe, or other handy implement. In such settings children learn by imitation that to give in to violent impulses is acceptable.

The ancient Greek philosopher Plato, through the persona of Socrates, in his dialogue *The Phaedrus*, expressed the problem of self-control in his allegory of the charioteer and the horses. A chariot is pulled by two horses, one light, the other dark. The charioteer tries to harness and train the horses to pull together and not against either the charioteer or each other. Though given many interpretations, Plato's allegory goes something like this: the charioteer is reason (our better self), the light horse is a drive toward honor and ambition, the dark horse is our appetites (for sex, money, and plain old stuff). A good life for Plato is one where these three elements of the human psyche are in a good balance, with reason taking the lead to harness ambition, needs and wants. When the horses are not trained, disaster follows as the psyche becomes unbalanced, heading off into foolish ambitions, or else addicted to money or sex or something else, and adopting strategies that only lead to hurt. Notice that Plato does not denigrate ambition or passion. He just suggests that untrained, ambition and passion will always lead us astray. When ambition and passion are controlled by reason we have self-control. A self-controlled life, according to Plato, is a happy life, a life of thriving and well-being.

A large part of the parental, and re-parental, task—if Plato is to be believed—is to help our children learn the skills of "charioteering," to keep their reason, ambitions, and passions in balance. We address reason more thoroughly in chapter five, but in this chapter we are looking more carefully at self-control, Steven Pinker's second "better angel."

Self-control, is in a sense, the flip side of empathy. With our better angel of empathy, we learn to feel for the Other, to realize to some extent what they face, and what will cause them harm. With empathy we feel with them and for them. With our better angel of self-control, we learn to keep a check on our impulses so that we don't cause harm to ourselves, or to others.

Van der Kolk helpfully suggests that:

> All mental suffering involves either trouble in creating workable and sat-
> isfying relationships or difficulties in regulating arousal (as in the case of
> habitually becoming enraged, shut down, overexcited, or disorganized).[4]

Workable and satisfying relationships rely, to a great extent, on the capacity
for empathy, while regulating arousal speaks to the necessity of self-control.
In other words, difficulties in these two areas require the development of
our two better angels of empathy, which we considered in chapter two, and
self-control, which we are considering here.

From our long term work with children, it's our view that these two better
angels are the most important to develop for ourselves, and critical to nurture
in the children we care for. Lack of empathy and self-control makes for a
more violent and harmful world. Children in care have likely not had empathy
or self-control modeled for them, and, hence not been taught how to feel
for others or to control their urges. Their lives are often, thus, a spiral of violence. Pinker comments, "Violence . . . is largely a problem of self-control."[5]

Self-control seems to be a matter of choosing to control those impulses
or desires that we know are not in our own best interests or the best interests of others. The possibility of choosing against what we know to be the
best has puzzled philosophers since Socrates. It is the problem of *akrasia,* or
weakness of will. In the New Testament, St. Paul in his letter to Romans
expressed the problem in this way:

> I do not understand my own actions. For I do not do what I want, but
> I do the very thing I hate. Now if I do what I do not want, I agree that
> the law is good. But in fact it is no longer I that do it, but sin that dwells
> within me. For I know that nothing good dwells within me, that is, in
> my flesh. I can will what is right, but I cannot do it. For I do not do the
> good I want, but the evil I do not want is what I do.[6]

St. Paul agonized with his experience of knowing the good but choosing the
bad. His solution was to think of his psyche as divided between his "self"
and "sin" that in some way dwells inside him, or perhaps between his mind
and his body. Certainly in popular Christian devotion St. Paul has often been
understood to denigrate the body as the source of human ills. The rationale
of the ascetic mistreatment of the body, often punishing the body, has been
on the basis that the body is the source of sin. In other words, the body is the
source of the weakness of will, the lack of self-control; bodily urges being
more powerful than the will to resist them. In this tradition, the body is also
associated with evil. If the weakness of will is a blame game, St. Paul is able
to shift the blame from himself to another entity. In other words, his choices
are beyond his control. His weakness of will is because of an overpowering
principle he calls "sin" that in some way is connected to his body.

Plato, in the persona of Socrates, addressed the issue some four hundred years before St. Paul, and arrived at very different conclusions. In the *Protagoras*, Socrates argues:

> So what we are saying then ... is that nobody ever willingly goes towards things that are bad for them, or even things they think are bad for them—it turns out that's an impossibility of human nature; to go towards things you believe are bad for you, willingly, instead of what you think is good; and nobody, if they're forced to choose between two things that are both bad for them, could ever choose the bigger bad thing if they're in a position to choose the smaller bad thing.[7]

Thus, at the moment of choice, I will always choose that which I believe to be in my best interests at that moment.

In days gone by, Andy was a runner. His favorite distance was the half marathon, and at just over 13 miles, it required a lot of preparation. Coaches in the 1980s suggested that to run an adequate half marathon, a runner would need to run 25–30 miles over a week, with some shorter and some longer runs. Andy knew this to be true, if he was to complete the course in a reasonable time. But on some days, the pleasure of reading a book, or sunbathing, or taking a gentle stroll with the family, seemed more appealing than a sweaty ten miles. The choice was the good of the run, and the long-term goal of the half marathon, or some other more immediate pleasure. Some days he chose the training run, and some days he chose the other activity. On those days he chose the other pleasure, was this a weakness of will, a case of *akrasia*? Not according to Socrates, who would likely say that Andy always made choices in line with what he perceived to be his best interests at the time. To choose a stroll in the park rather than a hard run was not weakness of will, merely a different choice based on reasons at the time. For Socrates, the will always acts in accordance with reason, and reason is about knowledge of that which is in our best interests.

Not all philosophers have agreed with Socrates. Even Aristotle, Plato's most famous student, distanced himself from the Socratic position. Where Socrates argued that the will always acted according to reason and best interest, Aristotle suggested the will was often guided by mere opinion—rather than true reason—and opinion could very well be wrong with regard to best interests.[8] In other words, the human agent does not always act totally rationally, and to assume so is folly. According to Aristotle, based on experience, people often make foolish choices, for their knowledge of their future best interests is limited.

Yet, it still seems to be the case that, even given the knowledge that something I do now will result in some long term bad, I may still do the foolish thing. In other words, I may act against reason. Behavioral economist George Ainslie suggested that this can be the case because people value something now rather than something later. He termed this the "hyperbolic discounting" model.[9] It is possible to discount future goods in favor of more immediate pleasures. For example, the long-term goal of weight loss does not seem as appealing as the pleasure of an extra piece of pie right now. However, people do not deliberate in every single decision but rather "bundle" decisions together. Philosopher Craig Hanson summarizes Ainslie's position on bundling as:

> Making one decision over a series of choices rather than unique decisions at every instance of a choice. So rather than going "Back to the drawing board" every time and re-evaluating, one makes a decision, a "rule," which one believes applies to a series of similar situations.[10]

This is not strictly speaking akratic behavior, a weakness of will, for a deliberate choice is made between a temporary pleasure now, and a long term good. It may be foolish to choose the immediate gratification, given possible futures, but such a choice is not necessarily a weakness of will.

*

Wilfredo came to us from a residential facility. He was a sixteen-year-old with a number of mental health needs. We had the unusual luxury of having the opportunity of meeting him before placement. He came to our house twice for a short visit before he moved in. Nevertheless, moving in with strangers, on whom you would be dependent for food, clothing and much more, must be terrifying. Will arrived early evening looking nervous and unsure of himself. As always, we did our best to put him at ease. He proved himself a likeable, chatty boy, although seemed to have developed no self-control or empathy for others. He took things without any thought for others. He knew it was wrong as he did it in a manner that was sneaky. Within the first week of placement he had stolen five times that we were aware of.

The things weren't of great value, nevertheless we knew it was a habit that needed to be broken. In another couple of years taking from others could get him into some fairly serious legal trouble. We did not want to see him become another teen who was heading for jail.

He took clothing and minor items from the other kids' rooms when they were out. He took all the snacks and drinks, often leaving the other three to find the cupboard was bare when they went to get a snack. When confronted with the evidence of his habit he denied it, becoming very angry, screaming and shouting at us.

We realized that the underlying problem was lack of self-control, plus some learned behavior from a very unstable family background and more than one residential facility. We had to find ways to help him develop self-control, moral restraint, and also empathy for those whom he was depriving by taking their possessions or share of the snacks.

*

What Plato, Aristotle, and Ainslie share in common is that the key to successful self-control is knowledge, understanding, and making the right choices.

Someone who works hard in seeking knowledge is more likely to know what are in her best interests and will likely act accordingly. Yet this does not seem to account for compulsions when a person feels they have no choice other than to act a certain way. The hyperbolic discounting model is likely most helpful, but still does not address the issue of addictive behavior. "I do this because I can do no other, even though I know it is not in my best interest." In other words, these thinkers do not account for addiction. And here we hit a roadblock, because the word "addiction" is used in many different ways in popular speech, not all of them helpful.

Contemporary analytical philosopher Lawrence Ashley suggests that what we commonly talk about as addictive behavior relates to either the ingestion of substances (drugs, alcohol) or the repetition of actions (video games, pornography). With regard to the former, the ingested substances create a change in the brain, as beta endorphins are released that create a craving. It is not as clear with regard to the latter, as substances in the blood stream have a more direct route to the brain than, for example, playing Xbox games. However, even here, studies have shown that such activity activates the pleasure circuits in the brain.[11] For Ashley, both ways of speaking about addiction—ingestion of substances or pleasure creating activities—are about the level of "resistibility." He suggests three broad areas of resistibility:

An addiction

A compulsion

A need

An urge

A self-indulgent choice

A habit, routine

An impulse

A whim[12]

The third set is the easiest to deal with. The middle set can be changed with some element of self-control (likely akin to Plato's chariot analogy). The first set "present genuine problems in terms of our freedom to liberate ourselves from them."[13] In other words, for Ashley, it is the first set in his hierarchy of resistibility that is truly addiction. Ashley is a thoroughgoing materialist, and he seeks to explain every human behavior as a physical rather than psychological problem.

In a sense, it matters not what descriptors Ashley places in his three sets of resistibility. What matters is that in the normal course of our lives some things are more resistible than others. We might as easily call these levels of resistibility "like," "want," and "need"; though we use "need" loosely.

Need in this sense is really "perceived need." Lisa, whom we considered at the beginning of this chapter, may have felt that she needed to be using technology all the time, but such a need is not the same kind of need as air, water or food, without which the agent dies. The person addicted to heroin, or alcohol, may feel that without a fix or a drink they will die—they need it—but we know that, though withdrawal is extremely unpleasant, it is not usually fatal. However, the point is that some actions we might "like" to take, or some substance we might "like" to ingest are easily put off. If our urge is a stronger "want," then to resist the action is more difficult, but doable with some persistence. But if the drive is more like a need, then such actions or ingestions will be the most difficult to resist. In the normal development of self-discipline, our likes and wants are the easiest to control through knowledge and understanding about our best interests, and the forming of good habits. To help children in our care understand their own likes and wants, and to moderate them according to good sense, is also the normal function of parenting as parents model self-control, and teach by explanation and exploration.

*

We like to watch British TV shows. These are often series of eight to ten episodes available to stream, and as the producers design the show, each episode in the series leaves us wanting more. The phase "binge-watching" has entered popular vocabulary. But that is where self-moderation comes in.

"Shall we just put on the next episode?"

"I really, really want to, it stopped at such an exciting place, but it's getting late."

"Yes, you are right, if we put on the next one it will be later than we normally go to bed when it finishes."

"We'd really regret it in the morning when the alarm goes off."

"Yes, we would. Put the television off."

*

This kind of normal process of considering our actions, weighing consequences and the ability to wait for something we want is all part of growing up. It is the self-moderation of what we would like to do, and what we know is not in our best interests. Sadly, it is a process many teens who have suffered violence, trauma and neglect lack. Helping teens to learn self-control is all part of the re-parenting task.

However, will these normal methods work when we are considering the strongest urges that amount to needs; in other words, when the actions or substances hold the power of addiction for ourselves and our children? Even more so, when the teen has a predisposition toward addiction, it becomes harder to learn self-control. Sadly, we have seen too many times that when a teen comes into our care with a family history of addiction, sometimes going back for generations, our child, too, leans toward addiction. Szalavitz comments:

Although people with addictions or potential addicts cannot be identified by a specific collection of personality traits . . . it is often possible to tell quite early on which children are at high risk.[14]

Of course, having a propensity to addictions does not mean that it is absolutely certain that a child will go that way. However, from our observation, the child will often struggle with both addicting activities and substance ingestion. As with most other human behaviors, the reason is likely both biological (genetics, heredity) and social (learning, imitating). In other words, a propensity toward addiction relates to both body and mind. Szalavitz comments with regard to her own addiction, "I'd soon find out that the question of whether body or mind matters more—and where the boundary between mind and brain, mental and physical is—runs through most of the key issues and fault lines in addiction."[15]

*

Chloe's parents had both struggled with alcohol as had their parents before them. They had not lived together since before Chloe was born. She lived with her mother and partner, and had very little contact with her father. Chloe was taken into foster care as a young teenager. She had seen the violence and harm caused in her family through alcohol abuse. Chloe was absolutely determined that she would never drink alcohol. She was a very intelligent girl and realized that alcohol could be her downfall. Throughout her teenage years she remained firm in her resolution even when she returned to live with her father. A few years later, as a young woman in her twenties, she was enticed to have her first drink. And another, and another, until she could no longer stand. Later she posted on her Facebook page that she knew that, for her, alcohol would always present a problem. Like Julie in Chapter 1, Chloe was a young person who ultimately was able to recognize her own propensity for addiction. She renewed her determination to avoid substances that she knew would be problematic.

Some do not find that sort of inner strength. These are teens who need nurturing in how to self-regulate or self-moderate their behavior. It seems like the addiction takes over and the teen has little control over themselves. This is something which has often not been learned as the teen is growing up. It is something that we exercise in everyday life all the time.

Many of the teenagers come to us with food issues. It is often the only area that can be in control in a life that feels like it is spiraling out of control.

*

Jamel had food issues which felt more severe. He had no self-control at all. We quickly saw the signs of a propensity toward addiction in the obsessive way Jamel collected things, but the food was something even we were unprepared for.

We had three boys in the house at the time, all unrelated. The other two were fifteen and sixteen years old, they were strong, tall boys. They seemed a lot older than Jamel, who had just turned thirteen. He still looked like a child. He was quite small for his age and preferred to play with younger children. The other two were kind to him but had little in common.

When Jamel was placed with us he was very overweight for his height and age. The doctor pronounced him obese and suggested a diet, complete with lots of information. We started him on a healthy eating program studiously avoiding the word diet.

It was moderately successful. Jamel started to lose weight in the recommended slow and steady way. The doctor was very pleased with his progress. However, Jamel continued to be addicted to food. There was no self-regulation, or impulse control. Everything on his plate was eaten. Sometimes we could see him struggling to force a mouthful of food down. We encouraged him to leave it if he was full. He always refused. With that in mind, we had to be careful to give him appropriate meals.

A few months after he was placed with us it was the Thanksgiving break from school. As we do every November, we hired a cottage at the beach for the five days. Being out of season the holiday town is always deserted. We get the long beaches to ourselves. It is a lovely break for us and a quiet time to take whatever children we have placed with us. It is great for them to experience the ocean in winter. All three boys loved the beach and seemed to have a good time. This year, with Jamel in mind, we mostly ate in our cottage. However, on our last day we decided to buy a takeaway for dinner as we had already started the process of cleaning the cottage for our departure.

We went to the nearest strip mall and decided on Chinese food. When we went in to the restaurant we found it didn't just serve take-away food, but had a few tables for people to dine in. The boys were all eager to stay and asked could we eat there. We agreed. It seemed easier and with the bonus there would be no washing up dirty plates at the cottage.

Each child chose the dish they wanted. We sat around chatting about what we had done during the previous few days. Then the meals were served. The portions were enormous! We don't think we have ever seen such big helpings, before or since. Rice was heaped like a mountain on each plate. Jamel stared wide-eyed at his huge plateful before tucking in. We watched him with horror. We were both thinking that this would not end well. It didn't!

Teenage boys can take a lot of filling, yet halfway through their meals two of the boys pushed away their plates.

"Jane, I can't eat any more," said Clinton. "I'm so full."

"Me too," chimed in Brady. "I feel bad about leaving so much though."

The two boys' plates were still over-flowing with food, as were ours. Yet all of us had eaten heartily.

Andy said, "Come on, Jamel, we are going to leave now. We have all eaten enough and we want to go back to have a last look at the moon shining on the ocean."

"No, I'm not going, I'm not finished and I'm not leaving my food." Jamel was clearly working himself up into a tantrum.

Jamel kept on eating. Each slow spoonful became an agony to watch. He was having to force the food down, and we could see how uncomfortable it was making him feel. We tried to persuade him to stop eating, even dangling the carrot of an offer of a take-away box so it could be eaten another day. Jamel started shouting that we wanted to steal his food. His lack of self-control was sad to watch.

Andy, Clinton and Brady went out to the car. We had learned, when Jamel was in a tantrum, the fewer people around the better.

Jane watched Jamel stuffing the food down as quickly as he could. He was clearly struggling to swallow. Jamel's stomach started to heave and Jane knew she had to intervene. She realized it would be harmful to let Jamel continue to eat. It was likely to make him really ill. A sick child on the seven-and-a-half-hour journey home would not be pleasant for anyone. Jane decided the best way was just to take a firm approach. She told Jamel that everyone had finished eating, it was time to go and find the rest of our party. In a swift movement, Jane took the plate and disposed of the remaining food.

Jamel screamed, "You stole my food! You stole my food!" Before Jane realized what was happening, she felt a sharp pain across the face. Jamel had hit her hard. A little embarrassing in a restaurant, and painful! Jamel ran out of the food outlet. Outside he became remorseful and full of apologies. He hadn't wanted to hurt Jane. His addiction was so great he had been out of control, unable to think about anything except food.

*

For philosopher Ashley, in simple terms, truly addictive behavior is not in the power of the addict to change, because addictive behavior is a product of changes in the brain caused by the ingestion of brain altering substances. In this, ironically, his analysis is not far removed from St. Paul's who insists that he cannot resist because of "sin that dwells within me," which for Ashley becomes not a sinful principle, but rather a change in brain state. St. Paul's idealism meets Ashley's materialism in the assertion that the power of choice is taken from the agent. St. Paul's solution is some form of divine intervention; that is, something outside the control of the agent. Ashley's solution is to rely on brain scientists to find a material solution to addiction through psychotropic medications, or else in some imagined future, by gene therapy. Any form of cognitive therapy—counseling, a twelve-step program—would ultimately not work for Ashley, for such remedies are categorically wrong. Trying to change minds is not possible when brains determine addictions. Thus, when we face the difficult re-parenting task in the face of addiction, Ashley's solution would be pharmacological, in the hope that a change in brain state would reduce the addiction.

But is Ashley's materialistic account correct? Philosopher Craig Hanson takes a mediating position between something like the Platonic, Aristotelian, Ainslian, position that knowledge and understanding will overcome addiction, and the Ashleyan materialist account of addiction. He argues for an acceptance of the hyperbolic discounting model, but allows, too, for the visceral—that is the physical, materialistic—nature of addiction.

Hanson concludes his analysis:

> Addicts are morally responsible, but not morally responsible for being addicts. They are morally responsible for what, in the light of their well-supported belief that they are addicts, they do or do not do. They are not morally responsible should they fail to overcome their addictions. Instead, they are morally responsible should they fail to try appropriate methods of doing so.[16]

Hanson's analysis is helpful in two ways. First, he deals with the moral condemnation that often accompanies addiction. Too often, people face criticism and judgment for being addicts. It's somehow their own fault. In our culture, we are in the strange position of viewing addiction as an illness, but at the same time offering a moralistic condemnation of the addict. Hanson rejects this, recognizing as Ashley does the visceral nature of addiction. But second, unlike Ashley's materialistic account, Hanson gives hope that, even given the visceral nature of addiction, there are steps that can be taken to help the addict overcome their addiction. This hope suggests that re-parents can take steps to help the children they care for, even when a "like" has become a "want," and has morphed into a "need."

Even so, in our experience, children whose self-control faces a "need"— an addiction—have presented one of our hardest challenges, and sadly we have cared for teens who have come with various addictions; the biggest four being drugs, alcohol, technology, and food.

Readers at this point may be wondering where the teenagers get all the money to purchase the technology on which they get hooked. Our first answer is: not from us! Although we have purchased technology, mainly tablets or phones as birthday or Christmas presents, we have never bought it routinely as a right. We do not pay phone bills, usually encouraging teens to use pay-as-you-go systems. Most of those allow unlimited texts, but limited calls and media.

Sometimes, birth parents will provide their kids with a phone, particularly if they are already on a family plan. Sometimes the teens will arrive with an Xbox or tablet. Once they are fourteen they will receive a very small monthly stipend from DSS. Prior to that we give them an age-appropriate allowance. We have known teens who spend the whole amount on phone cards and do so willingly.

Also, many of the kids work. There are several schemes that help teenagers in foster care get job placements. Often their wages are paid for by the organization as they gain work experience and build a resume. We are very appreciative of all the people involved in these various organizations. They work tirelessly to help and support teenagers in foster care. Our one concern is the amount of available money it puts in the kids' pockets.

This money serves to illustrate their lack of control. We encourage all the teenagers to save from their earnings. It can be a lot of money, especially during the summer vacation months. The teenagers still get their clothing allowance, so do not need to purchase clothing or shoes with their earnings. Some who are very fashion conscious do buy additional clothes, but most don't. We have many times wished that the organizations who paid them had some kind of mandatory saving scheme for a portion of their earnings. However, they don't, so we try to encourage the children that saving is a good practice to start. When they first start working we usually help them open a bank account. We suggest that they put half their money in a savings account, and the remainder in their general account. We talk about how they might want to buy a car or rent and furnish an apartment in the future. We are clear that it is their money, the savings would be in their names and they would be able to access it when needed. Most of the teenagers agree with us, they especially seem to like the idea of saving toward a future car. They even talk about how cool that will be, but their pay check is spent within days of receiving it. Even saving for a much wanted new game or new controller is impossible. Only one boy has ever actually taken our advice and had a savings account. He left our care shortly before he was twenty-one with a nice amount in the bank.

*

The big question remained, and remains still, how do we help teenagers find the sort of inner regulation that they need to be successful in their future?

Much has been written on the subject of self-moderation or regulation, but often about babies and toddlers. Self-regulation is something that usually starts to be learned in early life and continues as the young child matures. Yet, as re-parents we often take older children who have often never progressed in learning the skill. They don't know how to moderate their behavior. Part of the re-parenting task is to help these teenagers at least start to master self-control. Often, as in Lisa's case with technology, and Jamel with food, we have to impose an external help to keep the teen safe and healthy until they have internalized moderation.

But learning to moderate as a teenager is not easy. We have found that the younger they are, the more successful they have been. Thirteen- and fourteen-year-olds do better than those over fifteen. It seems that once they get a bit older they see foster care just as an imposition by the state to be endured. Many don't want help or to change their behavior. Yet there are exceptions, and we have been impressed how hard some teenagers have worked to manage to control themselves. We have seen teens over-come addictions to alcohol and drugs, anger, food and stealing. They have accepted the help from ourselves and, sometimes, from outside agencies.

*

Sixteen-year-old Connor came to us straight from rehab. His story was that he had been taken into foster care eighteen months earlier. However, the drug addiction had proved too strong and rehab had been suggested. After a rough start, Connor started to accept the help the program had offered him and did well. After a year, it was time for Connor to leave the center. Home wasn't an option so it was decided that he should re-enter foster care while preparing for an independent living program. Connor came to live with us and stayed for nearly a year.

Coming out of rehab is always a challenge. There are so many rules and regulations imposed to keep the young people safe so they are not exposed to the daily temptation of being able to obtain drugs. Although we have been told by several teenagers that it is possible to get drugs in these institu-tions, it is not easy. But re-entering the community, the teen returns to their old pattern of life: the same school, the same community. They will often run into their friends who may still be using drugs. They will need to have developed strong character and great determination to stay off drugs.

Connor was quite vulnerable. Underneath the tough outer appearance was a timid and shy young man. Would he be able to resist the temptations as he re-entered his old school and met his old friends? Connor was deter-mined. He was going to make it and he did!

*

Unfortunately, Isaac's story was very different. He, too, came to us after a lengthy stay in rehab. His story was different and the plan for him was ultimately to return home. We anticipated a placement of about three to six months with lots of visits home of increasing duration. Isaac was full of how well he was going to do. The first week he was with us he joined the YMCA with a commitment to get really fit. It was a good, healthy choice.

Then, Isaac met an old colleague. We knew that his friend had been part of his old life with drugs. It was a concern which we talked to Isaac about. We knew that peer pressure is one of the hardest things to resist. Isaac was determined to rekindle the friendship assuring us that he would help his friend stay off drugs.

Although we had only known Isaac a week, so hadn't really built a rela-tionship with him, it seemed that over the next few days his personality changed. A couple of days later we awoke to find we had been broken into. The windows in our finished basement were smashed. This is a big room, complete with bathroom, we use as our playroom/teenage "hang-out," complete with TV, games, books, etc. At first glance it didn't look as if much had been taken but there was some significant damage. We asked

Isaac and the other teenager living with us if they had heard anything or knew anything about the break-in. They both conveyed shock at the scene. We were not quite so convinced they were innocent, wondering if their friends were the culprits. It was not the first time we had been broken into, nor would it be the last. Each time there was a connection both to past foster children and drug addiction.

On this occasion, we called the police. A very astute officer arrived, she looked at the damage and immediately said she wanted to talk with both boys. She quickly dismissed our long-standing foster child and focused on Isaac. With her careful conversation, he quickly admitted that he had been responsible. Apparently, since the day he met his friend he had been leaving the house at nights to go and take drugs. We were horrified at how unsafe his behavior had been. He had opened the window at the top of the stairs, jumped onto our kitchen roof and then climbed onto the ground. All this so silently that it hadn't even disturbed our pugs. He had left a basement window open so he could re-enter the house in the early morning. The previous night, due to the level of drugs he had taken, he had mistaken which window he had left unlocked thus had forced a couple causing the window frames to break.

We were horrified at the thought of the injuries he could have sustained leaving our house, together with the level of drug addiction. After the appropriate authorities had been notified and the ensuing safety discussion had taken place, Isaac was returned to a rehab facility. In total, he had managed only three weeks in our home. This happened nine years ago at the time of writing. We did not hear from or about Isaac again. Then just last month Jane's attention was drawn to the name in headline of an article in the local paper. Isaac had been arrested on some very serious charges. It made sad reading especially as we remembered the eager young man who had arrived on our doorstep determined to do well. Sadly, addiction and peer pressure had won the day.

There is still much work to be done in finding ways to help traumatized teenagers overcome addiction. Our experience (and clearly that of Connor's former foster family) is that for many teenagers who have not been successful in a foster home, the root of the problem has been addiction to drugs or alcohol. Of course, that does not mean that all teenagers who have experienced drug and alcohol problems cannot do well in a foster home. Far from it, many are successful.

*

Generally, nurturing teenagers is hard. They are not babies who can be cuddled or young children who will often ask, "Can I have a hug?" Or "Can you brush my hair?"

Whenever we watched television in the evening we had one eleven-year-old boy who always asked, "Can I sit in the middle?" Such was his need for nurturing he craved physical touch and security. He knew (even subconsciously) what he needed, and asked for it in an appropriate way. He always wanted to sit between us, preferably touching on both sides!

However, as they reach the teenage years nurturing in such a physical way is much harder. Some teens still ask for a hug, but most don't want physical touch from strangers. As re-parents, we must try to find other ways to meet their need for affection.

Many teens have experienced codependency or relationship addiction as it is sometimes called. These relationships can be very destructive. Often when a child or teenager enters foster care they are physically parted. However, the emotional tie often remains. This manifests through behavior seen during visits, in phone calls or someone "just needing to drop something at the house" for the young person. Rarely, have we had the two people in a codependent relationship in the home together.

*

Jacinda and Jaquan were a brother and sister who were strongly co-dependent. We realized within a few minutes of meeting them. They could barely function without each other. It soon became clear that it was a very unequal relationship. When given a choice of breakfast foods or snacks Jaquan decided what they would both eat and drink. He wanted to choose his sister's clothes. He asked her to say she didn't want to continue in the summer camp she loved so he would not be parted from her. In his presence, Jacinda had no voice. It was concerning.

Yet even more worrying was the way the young man constantly touched his sister. She was tall, slim and looked much older than her chronological age. On sight, it would be difficult to realize that there was a huge six-year age gap between them. The physical touching raised some alarm bells. At times, it was so intense it felt embarrassing. If these had been unrelated teenagers we would have told them to cool it!

But these weren't two kids flirting. They were a brother and sister in a deeply concerning relationship. Their codependency was sufficient to cause many alarms. They were with us for only a very short amount of time. Jacinda barely spoke or offered an opinion in those weeks. Yet, the leaders of her summer camp program said that when she was there without her brother she was bright and talkative. She really enjoyed it.

Even in the short amount of time they were with us it was a challenge to know how best to respond to Jaquan's addiction to his sister. When she was out of the house he wandered around only waiting for her return. It was difficult to interest him in anything. He did not want to pursue a summer job or help at a camp. For us it made a lot of sense of the term relationship addiction. Jaquan had all the behaviors associated with addiction. It was going to be a long, hard struggle for him to learn some self-control around his sister.

Final Things We Have Learned

1.

First, we have learned that self-control is not easy! It's no wonder that philosophers since ancient times gave their attention to how to control our urges and appetites. If it was easy, or self-explanatory, they and we wouldn't be worrying and writing about it. Because it is not easy, we should expect difficulties along the way and not a few failures. And that's OK. If we realize this, then we can be forgiving with ourselves and remove ourselves from the blame game. Self-control is an important better angel, but its seeds in our psyche need to be developed, in just the same way as empathy. And, if it is so for the carer, it is equally so for the cared for. An overbearing and judgmental approach with the children we care for will be self-defeating. As these tender young lives develop, our first step in helping them develop self-control is to be forgiving of their faults and mistakes.

2.

We learned, for ourselves, to develop good habits of self-control, even in the little things. That is, we have paid attention to the way we speak and act. We have learned to be careful with words, for once spoken it is impossible to take words back. We have learned, too, to moderate our actions. For the Greek philosopher Aristotle, as for the Chinese philosopher Confucius, moderation in all things is a useful target to aim for. But, moderation requires self-control, and self-control requires the daily building of habits that refuse to move to excess. The development of personal self-control is essential as it leads to the third thing we have learned.

3.

Learning the habits, we model them for the children in our care. It's not helpful merely to tell children what they ought to do or not do. In this instance, they have to see self-control lived out before their eyes by their carers. It's only in the day to day modeling and demonstrating that children begin to imitate and learn self-control for themselves. We can model self-control in many little ways, those frustrating moments when someone cuts in front of us in the supermarket queue or tries to beat us from the red traffic light. We can speak aloud self-control, we can say that we can wait, we can show that we are not frustrated or angry.

4.

We have also learned not to allow the children and teenagers to "push our buttons." When a young person is placed in a foster home there is usually what is commonly known as a "honeymoon" period. Even though the children are grieving, everything is new and somewhat exciting. They get a nice room, new clothes, regular meals and outings. It is a whirlwind couple of weeks where all the attention is focused on the child. Then, reality seems to set in and often this is followed by a long period of "testing." During that time, the child seems to do everything they can to annoy the foster parent. These are often just little things, but many of them—a child who dawdles in the morning, thus missing the school bus so one of us is late for work or a child who always comes late for meals. The constancy of this behavior can be very frustrating. Of course, sometimes the "testing" is not so trivial, usually with teenagers who seem to want to see their foster carers out of control. We have often mused about whether this is a need to replicate their home circumstances. It usually takes the form of swearing at us, threatening us, and occasionally telling us to hit them! It is important for the re-parent to exercise self-control at all these times.

5.

When our children show signs of addiction to substances, it never hurts to seek professional help. But here we add a caveat. Professional help can be a mixed bag, especially with regard to substance use as too often moral opprobrium accompanies the help. Much in our culture assumes that people with addictions are morally to be blamed for what, in most other similar issues, is perceived to be an illness that requires care and concern, as well as treatment. The criminalization of drug use has caused untold damage, from social stigma to draconian jail sentences, for those who most need help. In chapter one, we considered the most common forms of treatment for troubled children as either therapeutic or pharmacological. It's clear to us that alongside such treatment there needs to be a safe and loving social support—in our terms loving nonviolent re-parenting—for treatment to be effective. Treatment based on shaming the sufferer for their illness works directly against such loving support. Care, then, is needed when considering treatment for addictions as not all professional help escapes the pitfall of victim-blaming. But such provides a helpful bridge to our consideration of Pinker's third better angel, moral sense.

6.

With younger children much of self-control is developed in learning to wait. We teach children to wait for their birthday presents, Christmas presents, or special treats. We refuse their pleas to open their gifts early explaining that by waiting the day will be more special when it arrives. Self-control is also learned by waiting for their turn at the playground or for their turn with a special toy in a play group. Playing games also helps children have self-control as they learn that they can't always win and don't need to be upset (or have a tantrum) when they lose.

Notes

1 Maia Szalavitz, *Unbroken Brain: A Revolutionary New Way of Understanding Addiction* (New York: St. Martin's Press, 2016), 64.

2 Ibid., 65.

3 Ibid., 65.

4 Bessel van der Kolk, *The Body Keeps the Score: Brain, Mind, and Body in the Healing of Trauma* (New York: Penguin, 2014), 81.

5 Steven Pinker, *The Better Angels of Our Nature: How Violence Has Declined* (New York: Viking, 2011), 592.

6 Romans 7:15–20, NRSV.

7 Plato, *Protagoras and Meno,* translated by Adam Beresford (London: Penguin, 2005), 358d.

8 Nicomachean Ethics, VII.1–10.

9 George Ainslie, "Hyperbolic Discounting," in *Choice Over Time*, edited by George Lowenstein and Jon Elster (New York: Russell Sage Publications, 1992); George Ainslie, "Hyperbolic Discounting as a Factor in Addiction: A Critical Analysis," in *Choice, Behavioral Economics and Addiction*, edited by Rudy E. Vuchinich and Nick Heather (Boston, MA: Pergamon, 2003).

10 Private email correspondence with Andrew Fitz-Gibbon, May 5, 2018.

11 M. J. Koepp, R. N. Gunn, A. D. Lawrence, V. J. Cunningham, A. Dagher, T. Jones, D. J. Brooks, C. J. Bench, and P. M. Grasby, "Evidence for Striatal Dopamine Release during a Video Game," *Nature*, vol. 393, no. 6682 (May 21, 1998), 266–268.

12 Lawrence Ashley, "Guest Foreword," in Craig Hanson, *Thinking About Addiction: Hyperbolic Discounting and Responsible Agency* (Amsterdam: Rodopi, 2006), x.

13 Ibid.

14 Szalavitz, *Unbroken Brain*, 59.

15 Ibid., 31.

16 Hanson, *Thinking About Addiction*, 93.

4 Nurturing Our Better Angel of Moral Sense

People should think less about what they ought to do and more about what they ought to be. If only their being were good, their works would shine forth brightly.

Meister Eckhart, *c.*1260–*c.*1328[1]

We should take seriously, then, the idea that we possess an innate and universal morality.

Paul Bloom, 2013[2]

The Case of the Disappearing Christmas Pudding

One of our local stores has a foreign food area, for which we are very grateful. We eagerly peruse the contents in the United Kingdom section each time we visit. It is not very big, just a set of shelving spanning a couple of feet. It gives us a small taste of home. We purchase foods that we miss—pickled onions, HP sauce, mint sauce, crumpets, marmalade, and British tea. Imagine our excitement when we visited at the beginning of December: stacked high on the shelves were Christmas puddings. Not only that, the labels proclaimed boldly, "suitable for vegetarians." They were exorbitantly priced, but we reasoned Christmas only comes once a year, and this would be our treat. We added one to our shopping cart and walked away, mouths watering. In the car, Jane spoke over the engine noise, "Do you think we should have bought two?"

"Well, they *are* really expensive," Andy responded with hesitation.

"But, we might not see them again for a while."

"I suppose it would be nice to have one at New Year."

"They might have all gone by next week when we shop again."

"And, then we'd have missed our chance!"

We turned the car around, and headed back to the store. Our second Christmas pudding was a little something extra to look forward to over the holidays.

Christmas pudding is a very heavy, steamed, rich dessert full of fruit which mainly includes raisons, currants, and sultanas together with many spices.

Traditionally it is served with brandy poured over it, which is set alight and the flaming pudding carried to the table. The pudding is the grand finale of the Christmas dinner and will be found adorning the tables of many households in Britain each year. The Christmas pudding has been around, in one form or another, since the fourteenth century. By the nineteenth century, its modern form had been more or less established. Charles Dickens mentioned it in his beloved book *A Christmas Carol*:

> In half a minute Mrs. Cratchit entered: flushed, but smiling proudly: with the pudding, like a speckled cannon-ball, so hard and firm, blazing in half of half-a-quatern of ignited brandy and bedight with Christmas holly stuck into the top. Oh, a wonderful pudding![3]

The Anglican Church's Collect—a kind of summary prayer that changes each week—for the Sunday before Advent (about the end of November) is "*Stir* up, we beseech thee, O Lord, the wills of thy faithful people; that they, plenteously bringing forth the *fruit* of good works" (italics ours). This Sunday is colloquially known as "Stir-up Sunday," and by tradition was the day when the pudding was made. Every member of the family would stir the pudding mixture before it was steamed and set aside, to be further steamed at Christmas time. As a child, Jane remembers well the tradition, before puddings were readily available in the stores. As society has changed, the practice of making one's own Christmas pudding has diminished, and now shop-bought ones have become the order of the day. Nowadays, puddings don't even need to be steamed—although that is the preferred method—just a few minutes in the microwave will suffice.

A few days after our purchase, Jane, rearranging the food cupboards went to add a few cans of beans to our pantry. As she walked away there was a nagging feeling that something was missing. She turned, reopened the door and saw the Christmas puddings were gone. Not just one, but both had disappeared! For a second Jane wondered had she put them somewhere else and forgotten where. Alas no! She realized quickly that they had been stolen. This was confirmed a couple of days later by finding one of the empty boxes that had been thrown behind a sack of potatoes.

Sadly, we knew which of the two fourteen-year-olds we were fostering at the time would be responsible. One of them had been stealing since she was placed with us, and many things had disappeared since Jessie had lived with us. None of the things taken was of significant value, mostly just little cheap trinkets, or packets of food, yet added together it amounted to a loss of several hundred dollars.

We had discussed stealing with Jessie many times in the few weeks she had been with us. Our mantra had become "if you need something, ask don't steal." We were faced with a dilemma: however much we talked about it, Jessie had never once admitted that she had taken things. Though she vigorously protested innocence, we had no doubt in our minds as some missing things turned up in her bedroom. Some were taken to school where a diligent teacher phoned us to check if she was supposed to have the items in question. Even months after Jessie left us, we would find bits of food, now rotten, and other missing objects in her hiding places—behind books in our library, under furniture, and in hidey-holes in the garden.

After her initial denials, Jessie quickly became violent and threatened to harm us, or the pugs. One of her common threats was that she would scratch the cars. Mostly, we let the minor issues go, and reserved talking to her only about the more serious items, or about items taken that belonged to our other foster children—mostly clothes and electronics. It was a clever strategy. First deny the thefts and then threaten violence, hoping that at the threats we would back off. The situation would escalate very quickly, and as we were seeking to help Jessie reduce her violence, we allowed much to pass unspoken. If we tackled every incidence, we would have engaged daily in the denial-violence-escalation cycle. Such would have been counter-productive.

Our dilemma was whether Christmas puddings were worth the violent escalation. Our suspicion was that Jessie would have taken one bite and thrown them away at school. We would not retrieve our Christmas treat. On the other hand, we knew Jessie needed to start to take responsibility for her behavior. We felt that only when she would admit to the habit, could we start to work with her to help reduce the stealing. On balance, in this instance, we decided to talk to her. Even though we were confident it was Jessie, our policy was never to accuse one child when anything went missing. So, as always, we talked to our two teenagers about the missing puddings.

"No, I don't even like Christmas pudding," said Zameer. "It was yuk." He had already been with us for a couple of Christmas Days and had not acquired the taste for the heavy fruit pudding.

"It wasn't me, I would never steal from you," Jessie added turning toward us with the wide-eyed innocent expression we had come to know well.

We chose in the moment to let it pass. We were content with, a few days later, saying how sorry we were that there was no British Christmas pudding with the Christmas meal. We then explained how it would have been cooked and presented at the table. Though a little sheepish, Jessie still did not own her behavior, regardless of the hurt she had caused.

By the time of the Christmas pudding incident Jessie had been with us for about three months. After this incident, we were proactive in trying to limit the stealing. We tried to minimize what Jessie had access to. We had already gained a good sense of what Jessie would take, so simply switched the contents of some cupboards around. This only had very limited success. We continued to miss items on an almost daily basis. Jessie still arrived home from school with electronics, and other things, that held teenage appeal. When asked where she had got them from the reply was always, "A friend gave it to me."

The big question was how to help Jessie develop a moral sense together with some empathy for those she had stolen from. Jessie had never had anyone to guide her. She had no basis for making decisions about right and wrong actions, and no sense that she might have caused harm. She had been socialized to focus only on herself, and her immediate needs, regardless of others. Although she never admitted stealing, she was aware that we knew what she was doing. Jessie seemed proud of her behavior, and had boasted on several occasions about the stealing done by her older siblings, even claiming that violence had been involved. She was quick to tell us, too, about extended family members who were in jail for theft with violence. Without the development of at least some basic moral sense, we could only foresee further problems down the road for Jessie. We are sure that others would not overlook her behavior as we had, and as Jessie matured into adulthood her lack of concern for others (demonstrated in her violence), and disregard of that which belonged to others (shown in her stealing) would bring unwanted and damaging consequences. In large part, Jessie's case is about a lack of moral awareness, but negotiating the terrain of morality is a tricky business.

What's the Good of Morality?

In contemporary American culture, morality has a bad rap, and for good reasons. Psychologist Steven Pinker states bluntly, "The world has far too much morality."[4] He goes on to explain that morality (like religion, with which it is often closely associated) has often become an excuse to do terrible things to others. In the name of religiously based morals people persecute others who differ, torture heretics, and murder unchaste sisters in "honor killings." Yet, even laying aside Pinker's extreme examples, people often think of morality as judgmental, stern, and critical of others. When morality enters public discourse, comments are mostly regarding sex and money, and little else. Watch for the words "moral lapse," "ethics hearing," or "ethics review board" in the media and you will likely read a story of someone who has flouted sexual mores, or else stolen the company's money in a dodgy financial dealing. So pervasive are such stories, that many of us are turned off issues of morality, and perhaps rightly so. Even so, Pinker admits that morality is also responsible for some of humanity's greatest achievements, such as the humanizing of social life during and after the Enlightenment in the eighteenth century, and the rights revolution of the last hundred years. He goes so far as to argue that the development of moral sense over the last 500 years has been a contributory factor in the overall reduction of violence. Morality, then, is a mixed bag.

Moralism and Relativism

For many years, Andy has taught ethics courses for undergraduate college students. Invariably, when students face moral philosophy for the first time—ethics and moral philosophy describe the same field in philosophy—they fall into one of two groups. Some students are either conventionally moral, often viewing morality as fixed, about rules and regulations, and with suitable punishments for moral infringements. Others tend to view morals as infinitely plastic, relativistic, and particular to each person. The two groups display the polar opposites of moralism and relativism. The moralist reacts against the relativist's apparent dismissal of morality. The relativist in turn reacts against the moralist's stricture and judgmentalism. It makes for interesting class discussions.

In conventional wisdom, a moralist is typically a busybody who takes delight in judging others' behavior and has a "holier-than-thou" attitude to life. In J. K. Rowling's *Harry Potter* book series, one of the main characters, Hermione Granger, is depicted in the first two novels as exactly this type of person. She is a rule-keeper, and constantly nags her friends, Ron Weasley and Harry Potter, to keep the school rules. Rowling paints Hermione as an unlikeable know-it-all—no fun at all! As the story progresses, Hermione's character softens as her persona changes. She remains the brightest witch in her school year, but becomes less judgmental, more compassionate, more willing to break the silly school rules for the sake of something better. In the process, Hermione becomes more likeable, and very much a role model for other young women to emulate. In Andy's college course, "Harry Potter and Philosophy," Hermione Granger is the character that many women in the class would like to be. In asking the students why Hermione is so attractive, it is not because she is a rebel, but because she is such a strong character. She is smart, compassionate, caring, and emotionally strong. If morality is only about sex and money, then Hermione's strength of character would be irrelevant. Yet, as we shall see below, there are better ways of thinking about morality than mere rule-keeping. The ethical, or moral question, since ancient times has been, "How shall we live?" Our English word "ethics," is derived from the Greek *ethos*, and "moral" comes from the Latin *mos*. They both mean the same thing. A person's *ethos*, or *mos*, was her way of living a good life—a life of well-being, of flourishing, for herself and those around her. In this sense, Hermione develops from being a rule keeper (a fairly rudimentary type of morality) to a deeply moral person, a person of deep character, or virtue, but in a very different sense to her former rule-keeping, busybody self.

Because of these problems with moralism, relativism might look like a good alternative, at least at first glance. Surely, it is better to allow people to choose their own morality, than to impose a morality based on someone else's worldview or religion? "Everyone is entitled to their own opinion," is a common response to ethical debate in Andy's ethics classroom. The sentiment is, of course, true. Freedom of thought, freedom of expression, is part of the cultural DNA of developed societies. However, such freedoms do not guarantee that every opinion is equally valid. Some opinions are better than others because they are based on a clearer understanding of the situation, have a better basis in reason, and can be argued more cogently (see

Chapter 5). When "everyone is entitled to their own opinion" is translated into ethical discourse, it becomes "everyone is entitled to their own morality," and the further leap, "and everyone's morality is equal to everyone else's." However, this is problematic. Just as some opinions are better than others, so some moralities are better than others, and for good reasons. The kindergarten teacher who cares for small children, out of a deep concern for their well-being, has a better morality than the child molester who repeatedly hurts children. The person of means who generously supports famine relief has a better morality than the person of means who steals from the poor in his neighborhood. So much is obvious, and is based on the common moral sense that it is better to help than to harm.

The move from "all are entitled to their own opinion," to "all are entitled to their own morality" faces two further problems. The first is that while everyone is entitled to their own opinion, in the United States based on the First Amendment, not everyone is entitled to their own morality. Societies created boundaries defining the limits of what is morally appropriate and what is not. The serial child molester might defend his behavior based on the freedom to assert his own morality, but society will not accept such a moral defense. In any given society, some moral positions are beyond the pale. That the boundaries of morality change over time, and differ between cultures matters not. In any particular culture, at any particular time, boundaries are set and people transgress the boundaries at their peril. Moral positions are debated at the boundary point, as cultural awareness shifts. That's to be expected. But no society could exist without at least some shared values, and these shared values define a general morality. No society is truly relativistic. The second problem, is that even those who espouse the moral relativist position, that all moral stances are equal, do not live as if their theory is true. Take the moral relativist's car without her consent and she will likely make an appeal to the wrongness of theft. Punch the moral relativist in the face and he will likely say, "You ought not to do that!" Moral relativists are only relativists in certain areas of morality. In truth, barring psychopaths and sociopaths, most people care about issues of justice and fairness, of causing harm, of compassion and cruelty. These are all moral issues.

If the media portrayal is to be believed, the United States is as polarized now as at any time since the Civil War. It's difficult to know the truth of this as the past often seems rosier than when it was experienced. Nonetheless, the "political" or "cultural" issues under debate that divide the nation are also, more often than not, substantial moral issues. They are moral issues because they are significant issues of "ought," or "ought not," that involve matters relating to harm and well-being. On whichever side of the debate one falls, whether people from other nations *ought* to be welcomed as residents and citizens is a moral issue. Whether an unborn child *ought* to be given the same human rights as a child after birth is a moral issue. So, too, is whether men *ought* to make decisions about the bodies of women. All the major "hot button" topics of our cultural discourse are moral issues, and people care deeply about them.

Of course, not all "ought" or "ought not" issues are moral issues. When my *ought* affects only me, then it is likely not a moral issue. Trivial issues of *ought* and *ought not*—whether I *ought* to buy another pair of shoes, whether I *ought not* upgrade my cell phone as soon as the new one comes out—are of a different kind. What makes the difference? Moral issues of obligation usually involve harm, justice, disrespect, and the well-being of others.

Still, if moral issues, then, are the serious *ought* and *ought not* issues we face, that affect the well-being of others, then the scope of morality is quite wide. It's easy to see this returning to the Harry Potter story, and likely most other stories that grip the imagination. Readers care deeply about the moral issues expressed in the story, though not often expressed as such. When Hermione is tortured by Bellatrix Lestrange, readers feel for her, and become indignant at her treatment. When Professor Snape arbitrarily takes points away from Griffindor House in the race to win the House Trophy, readers sense the injustice of it. When the evil Lord Voldemort meets a sticky end when his killing curse backfires, readers feel that justice has been served. And when Harry Potter's aunt and uncle mistreat and neglect him— punish and scold him with words and hands, clothe him poorly in too-large hand-me-downs, and keep him locked in the cupboard under the stairs— readers know how wrong the Dursley's are in doing so. All these are moral issues because they involve the *prima facie* obligation not to cause harm to others, not to act unfairly, and positively to respect others.

In terms of our subject—the treatment of children in care—it is clear that the issues we are dealing with are serious moral issues, and more than just "social" issues. That parents *ought not* subject their children to neglect or mistreatment is a moral issue. That parents *ought* to provide a safe and nurturing environment is a moral issue. Whether the authorities *ought* or *ought not* take children into care when faced with neglect or mistreatment in the birth home is a moral issue. That re-parents *ought* to provide a loving nonviolent home where children can heal from their trauma is a moral issue, too. In all of this we are considering what is fair for children, and, also, what a life of well-being, or flourishing, would be like. We are concerned with how we *ought* to care for children who have been subjected to violence and through that violence have been traumatized.

Not Quite a Blank Slate—Babies and Moral Sense

But let's back up a little. It has become quite common to assume that moral sense comes from our upbringing and socialization. To oversimplify, humans are born as a *tabula rasa*, a blank slate. We learn from our parents, and then from society at large through education and media. In other words, morality is mostly about nurture, and not very much about nature. Some psychologists have reason to suggest otherwise. Steven Pinker, besides writing about how violence has declined over the last half millennium, has earlier written extensively about the "nature or nurture" debate.[5]

To simplify: a trend in academic scholarship, now adopted generally, has been to suggest that biology, genetics, or nature have little to do with human behavior. The way we turn out as adults has everything to do with nurture, the socialization process we undergo in our families, schools, and through society generally. Pinker calls this trend "the modern denial of human nature." He suggests such is a major mistake and argues that both biology and sociology have important parts to play in human development. But he does not argue for a bland middle ground, that all human behavior is partly biologically determined, and partly socially constructed. His position is more nuanced. Some human behavior is mostly about biology (the drive to reproduce, for example), and some mostly socially constructed (whether long hair or short hair is more appealing in the courtship process). What is clear, and a necessary corrective, is that human nature does exist, that universals can be found, and that they are held in common by most cultures. In an appendix, Pinker cites hundreds of such universals demonstrated by the cognitive sciences.[6]

More recently, in *Just Babies*, Paul Bloom presents evidence to suggest that human babies are born with a rudimentary moral sense. He proposes that "certain moral foundations are not acquired through learning."[7] This moral sense is a product of biological evolution, and is much closer to a gut feeling than it is to a reason why something is considered right or wrong. Bloom cites a number of studies when very young babies are given simple tests of "nice" and "nasty" interactions with adults (sometimes using puppets). For example, in a simple puppet show, the baby's attention would be drawn toward a helping character, rather than a hindering character. The babies' reactions—attention span, facial expression, simple choices like reaching for the helping character—mimicked what in adults we would consider moral choices. Bloom says:

> These experiments suggest that babies have a general appreciation of good and bad behavior, one that spans a range of interactions, including those that the babies have never seen before . . . the babies' responses do have certain signature properties of adult moral judgments.[8]

Experimental psychology is adding weight to ideas that were common during the Scottish Enlightenment in the eighteenth century. While much philosophy has considered moral sense as a function of reason, of weighing in the balance the merits of good and bad choices, of providing reasons why some actions are morally good and some bad, Scottish philosophers suggested that morality was more about feelings than thoughts.

Adam Smith, most famous for his 1776 book on political economy *The Wealth of Nations*,[9] considered his earlier work, *The Theory of Moral Sentiments*, the foundation for his later book. Though known as the father of modern capitalism, Smith believed that a capitalist economy could only function for the good in a well ordered and moral society. First published in 1759, Smith opened his book with the following words:

> How selfish soever man may be supposed, there are evidently some principles in his nature, which interest him in the fortune of others, and render their happiness necessary to him, though he derives nothing from it, except the pleasure of seeing it.[10]

He argued that morality is not so much about coming to a reasoned position about right and wrong behavior, but is rather innate in human beings as social animals. In other words, moral sense is a natural aspect of being human. Specifically, the natural moral sentiment consists in sympathy and benevolence. Human beings are empathic animals, rooted in their sense of self—everyone cares for themselves—and their connectedness to others. We naturally want to do to others what we would want them to do to us. Smith expresses it:

> When we see a stroke aimed, and just ready to fall upon the leg or arm of another person, we naturally shrink and draw back our own leg or our own arm; and when it does fall, we feel it in some measure, and are hurt by it as well as the sufferer.[11]

Smith here foreshadows the work by psychologists in the area of mirror neurons that we touched on in *Welcoming Strangers*. His work, based on the close observation of human experience, was a direct challenge to those views of human nature (typically Thomas Hobbes) that suggested that people were aggressive by nature.

Smith's ideas were similar to those expressed by fellow Scottish philosopher, and friend, David Hume. In 1751, Hume published his *An Enquiry Concerning the Principles of Morals*.[12] Like Smith, Hume followed the principle of the "experimental method": deducing general maxims from the examination of particular instances.[13] His conclusion was that our moral sense is a product of sentiment rather than rationality. To simplify, we "feel" rather than think morality. When we see the bully hit the smaller person, we do not think "that is morally wrong," but feel it at a visceral level. We sympathize with the bullied and respond internally before applying rationality. To be sure, after the event we might give thought as to the rightness or wrongness of the action, but at the point of experience, we feel moral sentiments rather than think moral thoughts. Hume went so far as to say, that "Reason is, and ought only to be, the slave of the passions, and can never pretend to any other office than to serve and obey them."[14] In other words, feeling is primary, and is more like hunger, thirst, or physical pain than it is a rational process. For Hume, moral sense is like that.

Hume was correcting a long-held understanding that morality was a function of rationality, and that rationality belonged to the human animal only. Human beings, created in the image of God, share God's rationality. Though humans share aspects of animality, they are more god-like than animal-like. "You have made them a little lower than the angels," declared the Psalmist,[15] and this "little lower" clearly made the human considerably higher than the animals. Though the other animals did not share rationality, humans being "flesh" shared corporality with the animals. Mind and spirit were valued, and the body largely denigrated. As passions (in Hume's terms) were more animal-like, religion and philosophy considered the passions an aspect of the lowest and meanest human reality. Hume helpfully corrected this viewpoint, reconnecting humanity with its animal reality in a good way. The passions were a primary human experience. Reason was to be passion's slave.

Like most corrections of an imbalance, it becomes easy to shift too far in the opposite direction. We understand now that reason and feeling are intimately connected in the human psyche. Though feeling is visceral and intimately connected to the body—heart rate increases, "butterflies" in the tummy, embarrassed flushes, and adrenalin for instance—and we feel before we think, feelings are also connected to reason. We feel a certain way because we think certain things. The vegan who has thought deeply about animal rights will feel differently, when seeing video of an animal prepared for slaughter, than the meat eater who thinks differently. Habits of thought undoubtedly affect the way we feel. Nonetheless, Hume's was a necessary corrective to the over-emphasis on reason in determining moral sense.

For our purposes, the views of Smith and Hume suggest that however poorly children have been cared for, and however buried moral sense might be as result of violence and trauma, deep inside remain the foundations of sympathy and benevolence. In other words, we have something to work with. Further, we are working with the grain of nature and not against it.

Nonetheless, the sad truth is, in our experience many of the children we have cared for have a very limited moral sense. Doubtless this is caused in part by inadequate parenting, and in part by the trauma induced by violence. Those who ought to have nurtured and developed moral sense in these children, have often instead damaged the natural, but frail, moral sense that very young children have. Our task is to help our children rediscover, and then develop, what Smith and Hume characterize as sympathy and benevolence.

Virtue Ethics—A Different Perspective on Morality

Adam Smith and David Hume had tapped into an ancient stream of thinking about morality. Ethics is more about the kind of person I am, than about any single moral choice. We touched on this in *Welcoming Strangers*, helping the reader see how important loving nonviolent character is in caring for traumatized children. In developing Hermione's persona, J. K. Rowling, too, tapped into this ancient way of thinking about morality. To be a moral person is to be a person of strong character—what the ancients called virtuous—who is not tied to trivial rules and regulations. The virtuous person does the right thing, seeks the best for others, and lives the best life because she is *that kind of person*. In ancient philosophy, morality was not merely about sex and money, but about answering the questions, "How shall we live?" and "What would a good life look like?"

In *Welcoming Strangers*, we focused on the type of virtue ethics developed by the Greek philosopher Aristotle. In brief, you become a virtuous person by repeated acts of virtue. A courageous person becomes such by the daily, and often small, acts of courage. Over time, courageous habits make for a courageous person. The person who has habituated courageous acts will most likely act courageously in a time of stress. A loving nonviolent re-parent becomes such through countless loving nonviolent actions, habituated daily in the care of children, and, truthfully, in the whole of life.

However, there is another ancient form of virtue ethics, with similarities to the Aristotelian kind, but with other helpful insights. One of the key influences in the development of Chinese culture, Confucius, considered a good life to be one of humaneness. Like Aristotle, Confucius taught that to live a good life required quite a lot of hard work. In Confucian terms, this required the practice of *li*, or rituals, that in time shape character. Michael Puett and Christine Gross-Loh characterize these Confucian habits as "as-if rituals."[16] For Confucius, personality and character are not unchanging, as if fixed in concrete. Human beings are malleable, and we can change the way we behave and respond through daily mundane habits that make us better people. Puett and Gross-Loh state, "Over time you internalize a more constructive way of acting in the world instead of being led by your undisciplined emotional reactions. Little by little you develop parts of yourself you never knew existed, and you start becoming a better person."[17] In other words, for Confucius and the Chinese sages, as for Aristotle and the Greek philosophers, by acting "as-if" you are a certain kind of person—courageous, kind, loving—in time you become that kind of person.

Yet, habits can be helpful or hurtful. When our habits are unintentional—ways of behaving we pick up without being aware of them—they can hinder our well-being and that of others. When we first came to the United States in the mid-1990s, we both unconsciously adopted new eating habits. American portions were so much larger than we had experienced in the United Kingdom. The new habits came at a cost: we both put on weight. After several years of new eating habits, we realized the problem and intentionally had to change our habits. We can pick up, too, unconscious and unhelpful habits in the way we relate to others. Constant criticism, back-biting, gossiping, and finding fault, when habituated make you much less than you could be. Parents, too, easily habituate ways of relating to their children in words and actions that inhibit the child's flourishing, and if not checked, cause harm. Puett and Gross-Loh again: "Our patterned behaviors and rote habits—not rituals [in the Confucian sense]—are what really dictate our lives and get in the way of our caring for other people."[18]

In other words, the unintentionality of rote habits needs to be replaced by the intentionality of "as-if" habits, what we have characterized as the habits of loving nonviolence. And the habits begin in small ways. "Change doesn't happen until people alter their behavior, and they don't alter their behavior unless they start with the small."[19]

Making Principles Out of Commandments

Over the years, likely as most readers, we have been accused, judged, and have felt the sting of the morally self-righteous. Morality is easy to dismiss if we equate it with judgmentalism and self-righteousness. Such "morality" is unhelpful: it ruins relationships, and, as Pinker points out, can become an excuse for all manner of harms. No wonder many want to leave moralism behind, and prefer a view that sees morality as relative. Each person's morals are their own business, and, further, each person's morals are equally as valid as anyone else's. Understandable though such a reaction is, it is neither helpful for society, nor close to the reality of people's everyday lives. We have already demonstrated that, when our understanding of morality is broadened to include human well-being and flourishing, then morality affects us all, whether we like it or not. To think of the moral life in terms of character, as we have demonstrated in the virtue ethical approach, is more helpful.

However, we are aware that some readers, and re-parents, will want to maintain a more traditional and conventional understanding of morality based on rules of appropriate behavior. For such readers, we offer below an affirmation of conventional morality, but with a proviso. As we have seen, conventional morality can all too easily wear the clothes of judgmentalism, with its associated strictures and punishments. When we take such a moral view into caring for traumatized children, the strictures and punishment do more harm than good. The child is reinforced in their experience of the world as an unfriendly place where adults cause hurt. After all, much corporal punishment is administered on the basis of just deserts. The notion that bad children ought to be punished remains strong, though with little thought behind the practice. It's a parent's moral duty to punish a child, so the story goes. But, when a re-parent takes that stance, the child's trauma is reinforced rather than healed.

Our proviso with regard to conventional morality is that, rather than relying on strict rules, we can abstract principles from traditional morality that are more flexible and nuanced—less likely to be used as a rod with which to beat others. These principles can act as guides to us, pointing us in the right direction, but not as a point of criticism and judgment of others who do not match our ideals. In this we are venturing into a fruitful area of moral philosophy termed "principlism." Scottish philosopher W. D. (David) Ross first suggested this way of thinking about morality back in the 1930s. Later, it was developed further by medical ethicists Tom L. Beauchamp and James F. Childress.

Ross coined the term *"prima facie"* or "conditional" duties.[20] Duties are obligations: something that we ought to do. They are *prima facie* because they apply if no good reasons can be found for them not to apply. They are conditional because they are context dependent. Sometimes conditional duties may be in conflict with each other, and one duty may be overridden by another. Because principles are context dependent, some skill is needed in their application, rather than the stilted and unthoughtful following of rules. Ross suggested six broad areas:

1 Obligations connected to some action. He divided this into two: fidelity, where I have promised to act in a certain way; and reparation, where I have committed a wrong that needs to be made right.
2 Obligations of gratitude, when a kind action has been taken toward me.
3 Obligations related to the distribution of pleasure or happiness, that is, the principle of justice.
4 Obligations of beneficence, where I can increase the pleasure of others.
5 Obligations of self-improvement.
6 Obligation of not harming others.

Though Ross called these six "obligations," in the way he uses the word it is better to think of them as principles, as opposed to unbreakable rules. From Ross's obligations, we can suggest the principles of keeping promises, righting wrongs, being thankful, being fair, doing good, improving yourself, and not harming others. In many respects these principles have the feel of conventional morality, but without the censoriousness of rules, with punishments for rule-breaking. It would be easy to imagine how life would flourish if we took these principles seriously.

Beauchamp and Childress simplified the principlist approach for medical ethics, and reduced the six principles to four, using three of Ross's, non-maleficence (not doing harm), beneficence (doing good), and justice, and adding one Ross did not consider, autonomy.[21] To look at ethics in this principlist way is to make morality less certain, less clear cut, and more flexible in application depending on the complexities of circumstances. Though Pinker does not say so in *The Better Angels of Our Nature*, it is likely these *prima facie* obligations are the heart of why the moral sense developed in the last 500 years has contributed to the decline in violence. Our suggestion is that these principles applied to the care of children will reduce violence in the home, and contribute to the well-being and healing of children traumatized by violence.

Of interest is that the principles identified by Ross, and Beauchamp and Childress, can be found in most of the world's religious and philosophical traditions. In other words, they are not particular to any culture or worldview, and can be discovered in all. With a little careful thought, something like these principles can be abstracted from most ancient and modern moral codes—but abstracted in such a way that the peculiarities of context are not a barrier to relevance in our current context. Below we consider two ancient moral codes to show how, what are often taken as rigid rules, may point toward *prima facie* ethical principles.

Perhaps, the most obvious example is the Ten Commandments, drawn from the Jewish tradition, and often accepted by Christians as a standard of moral behavior. In recent cultural debate, the Ten Commandments have become an issue to divide further the nation. Conservatives argue that the United States was built on the foundation of such religious moral ideas, and that it is acceptable to, for example, display prominently the Ten Commandments in court houses. Liberals suggest, given the constitutional separation of religion and state, and the fact of a multi-religious citizenry, it is inappropriate to have symbols that favor one religion in public spaces. In the internecine tug-of-war, something very important is lost. On the one hand, it is clear that, even given a casual reading, the Ten Commandments contain details and issues largely irrelevant to many people in the modern world. We don't have much need for donkeys these days, nor accept the abhorrent idea of slavery and owning people, while Sabbath keeping is a minority practice. On the other hand, if the general moral principles offered in the commandments are rejected on the basis of its particular religious and cultural context, we miss something important.

Most commentators on the commandments suggest that they may be divided into the "religious" commandments and the "moral" command-ments. The "first table" is only helpful to those who share the religious view expressed in them—worshipping God, observing the Sabbath Day, for example. If we set aside these commandments that relate specifically to religious practice, the second six give us clues as to the kinds of *prima facie* moral principles we might want to develop in ourselves and our children. Here are the six, in their traditional form:

- Honor thy father and mother.
- Thou shalt not kill.
- Thou shalt not commit adultery.
- Thou shalt not steal.
- Thou shalt not bear false witness against thy neighbor.
- Thou shalt not covet thy neighbor's wife, servants, animals, or any-thing else.

We are not suggesting that these six, as traditionally given and in their ancient context, are without issues. For example, derived from a patriarchal culture, in their original form the commandments were written to straight males only. We realize this when we reach the last commandment and discover that to covet a neighbor's wife is morally wrong. Only males are addressed. Presumably, then, women are free to covet their neighbor's hus-bands with impunity! And in the age of marriage equality, would a gay man be free to covet his neighbor's husband, whereas a lesbian might break the commandment if she covets her neighbor's wife? Further, this command-ment suggests that women, as well as servants—which in the context meant slaves—were merely property. Men owned things, including women and slaves. Women and slaves were not counted as people worthy of address-ing in the commandment. Further, to ask children to honor their parents becomes problematic when parents are abusive. On the basis of the com-mandment, women and children have too often been enjoined to obey abusive males. A literal reading of the commandments, as unbending moral rules, then has its problems.

Nonetheless, from these ancient commandments we can derive the following principles: respecting others, refusing violence, being faithful, respecting that which belongs to others, telling the truth, and not being jealous of what others have. Such principles, while being derived from the commandments of conventional morality, are more flexible, context dependent and not tied to any particular religious worldview. In fact, with-out something like these *prima facie* moral principles, social life becomes precarious, harsh, and uncertain.

Our second example comes from the Zen tradition. Buddhism, like all the world's great traditions, is extraordinarily complex and variegated in its expressions. In the Mahayana tradition, Chan (in China) and Zen (in Japan) place emphasis on the ten vows of the Bodhisattva. Though expressed dif-ferently by different sects, this version is typical and comes from the San Francisco Zen Center:[22]

1 A disciple of Buddha does not kill but rather cultivates and encourages life.
2 A disciple of Buddha does not take what is not given but rather culti-vates and encourages generosity.
3 A disciple of Buddha does not misuse sexuality but rather cultivates and encourages open and honest relationships.
4 A disciple of Buddha does not lie but rather cultivates and encourages truthful communication.
5 A disciple of Buddha does not intoxicate self or others but rather culti-vates and encourages clarity.
6 A disciple of Buddha does not slander others but rather cultivates and encourages respectful speech.
7 A disciple of Buddha does not praise self at the expense of others but rather cultivates and encourages self and others to abide in their awak-ened nature.
8 A disciple of Buddha is not possessive of anything but rather cultivates and encourages mutual support.
9 A disciple of Buddha does not harbor ill-will but rather cultivates and encourages lovingkindness and understanding.
10 A disciple of Buddha does not abuse the Three Treasures but rather cul-tivates and encourages awakening, the path and teaching of awakening and the community that takes refuge in awakening.

Even given a casual glance, it's easy to see how moral principles might be abstracted from these precepts of Zen Buddhism, without adopting the religion or philosophy of Zen. Such principles would include respect for life, and especially for all people, respect for that which belongs to others, and commitment to nonviolence. Again, this ancient wisdom shares a synchronicity with the moral principlism of Ross, Beauchamp and Childress, and with principles abstracted from other traditional formulations, such as the Ten Commandments.

Further examples could be given, but even with these two it becomes apparent that something like these principles can be found in all the worlds' philosophical, cultural and religious traditions. For example, honor and respect have always been important principles in Chinese society, based on the teachings of Confucius. Nonviolence and refraining from killing have been significant in the cultures of southeast Asia. When we flout these basic moral principles, we store up trouble, if not immediately, then certainly in the long term. Without these moral principles we open ourselves to that which is vicious and cruel. Common to all these principles is a way of living that facilitates good and healthy human interactions; in other words, a moral life directed at empathic and caring relationships.

Modeling a Good Life for Children

For the re-parent the big question is how to develop moral sense in those who have not had any early teaching in right and wrong. This is exacerbated when a child has been actively taught to develop unprincipled and unhelpful habits.

*

We took a sibling group of three girls whose ages ranged from ten to thirteen. A few weeks after they had been placed with us they accompanied us on a trip to the shops to buy food. After we had placed a few items in our shopping cart Katie, the youngest, piped up, "I can teach you how to get some more cookies."

We asked her what she meant.

"Well, my mom taught us how to take things off the shelf and hide them in our clothes."

"Yes, that way you don't have to pay," added her sister.

Katie continued, "The stores have too much food, so it is okay to take what you need."

The eldest child quickly tried to tell her younger sisters to stop talking. She, at least, knew that taking things from the store was wrong, though her concern was more about getting her parents in trouble, rather than the wrongness of taking what does not belong to you. However, neither of the younger two had any idea that they should not steal. On this occasion, we just listened. To tell a child that something their birth family had taught them was wrong is never helpful. Teaching the girls about respect for what belongs to others would be part of many other conversations at later dates.

*

Jane was doing the ironing, a seemingly endless task in a home with many teenagers.

"Andy, I'm a little worried about all these new clothes that keep appearing in DeQuan's laundry. I know he has that little after-school job, and does use his wages to buy extra clothes. But these are designer labels, I don't think he could possibly afford them all."

"We should keep an eye on that and if it continues we can talk to him when the opportunity arises. He may just have found some good bargains."

"I know. I don't want to accuse him. But I have to admit I'm concerned."

DeQuan was a very pleasant older teenager. He had done well in foster care. He received good grades at school and was well thought of by staff, and peers, alike. Unfortunately, a few days after our conversation he and a friend were picked up at a local mall for stealing. It transpired that his friend's parent had schooled the boys in shoplifting. We were concerned he had succumbed to peer pressure. Over the few years he had lived with us, DeQuan had developed a strong moral sense. He was aware he had done wrong. He even shed a few tears over the incident that resulted in a court appearance. Fortunately, as it was a first offense he was merely given a warning. It was sufficient. DeQuan had suffered a lot of inner turmoil due to his lapse in moral sense. We don't believe he ever did it again. Certainly, after graduation he went to college and has since entered the workforce.

*

These two stories show the difficulty of the task for a re-parent in helping children develop a moral sense. DeQuan had really made great progress, he knew what he was doing was wrong. He felt guilty while taking things. Nevertheless, peer pressure had proved stronger than the budding moral sense he had developed.

In the sibling group, the youngest two girls had no sense of right and wrong and were surprised that some of the things they did were considered wrong. Their elder sister had an inkling it was wrong and was embarrassed by her siblings' conversation. Although we recognize had we not been present she would have taken the cookies, it was encouraging to see the seeds of a moral sense. From later conversations, we became aware that many times the girls had stolen food from stores because they were hungry. In those circumstances, we too might have taken food! It's a complex issue, but the last thing these children need is further blame and shame. We have found little lasting fruit in addressing an issue in the heat of the moment as a means of changing or preventing the action reoccurring. Of course, it is often necessary to talk to a child in the immediacy of their behavior, but even here gentleness and consistency are required rather than accusation and punishment. It is the ongoing conversations, and modelling a different way, that start to bring about change in thought and behavior.

*

While shopping one day, Jane calmly asked our twelve-year-old, Marley, to return the coloring book and pens she had pushed up her sweater. The bulky items were not well disguised! Marley started to scream, bringing onlookers from various parts of the store. It was not an edifying moment as the tantrum continued for several minutes. Eventually, the items were replaced on the shelves and our child left the store still screaming. A few minutes later Jane reached home with a happy smiling child who seemed to have already forgotten the tantrum. Marley agreed, during the ensuing conversation, that taking the items was wrong. That was, until the next time: Marley continued to steal. We have never had an expectation that long developed habits will change because of one incident. Much of what we do we think of as planting seeds of a moral sense which we hope will continue to grow long after a child has left foster care.

*

Our concern in *Nurturing Strangers* is not morality generally, but rather how this might help those of us who are re-parents to care for children who have been victims of violence. Steven Pinker's argument is that moral sense is one of the four better angels that have contributed toward the pacification of society, and the reduction of violence over the last five hundred years. On all counts, we are less violent and safer than we have ever been. It seems counterintuitive, given the prominence of violence in the news, but the data are impressive. In his latest book, published as we were finishing the manuscript for this book, *Enlightenment Now*, Pinker takes a new look at his dataset, and the trends still hold. The world has been free from major conflicts between the major powers, incidents of genocide are in decline, as are homicide deaths.[23] The fate of children is now far better than ever it was. Pinker comments, for example, "how common infanticide was in human history. From time immemorial, parents have abandoned, smothered, strangled, beaten, drowned, or poisoned many of their newborns," and that our cultural heritage tells of other egregious treatment of children.

On a recent visit to the U.K. we were walking the Cumbrian Coastal Path in the northwest. Whitehaven is a former coal town, boasting the earliest and deepest pit. Along the path lies the old ruin of Salton Pit, now inaccessible because of erosion of the cliffs. The mine, first sunk in 1729, had a shaft six metres above sea level, was 146 metres deep, and ran out to sea two kilometres. Children, as young as nine years old, would work a twelve-hour shift in the pitch black with no candles. A plaque commemorating the mine quotes an ancient miner, "On their first introduction to the mine the poor little victims struggle and scream with terror at the darkness."

We have certainly moved a long way from such now unthinkable treatment of children. Nonetheless, there is still work to be done. Pinker's analysis does not mean that our culture is violence free, nor that certain vulnerable members of society do not suffer terrible violence and its ensuing trauma. As we demonstrated in an analysis of the data in *Welcoming Strangers*, though the trends are positive, children still do suffer in large numbers at the hands of their caregivers. If the better angel of moral sense has helped in a general way in the reduction of violence, how might it help specifically in the reduction of violence against children in care?

We suggest in two ways. First, carers internalize the morality of loving nonviolence, both in the principlist sense of using the prima facie principles as a guide, and in the habituation of loving nonviolent actions to create loving nonviolent character. (We are using "habituation" in the positive sense of building good habits, and not in the psychological sense of boredom, or the response to sameness.) In this way, re-parents prepare themselves to care in the best way for children traumatized by violence. Second, by becoming exemplars and models of loving nonviolence to the children they care for, re-parents can help children develop this moral sense too.

The principlist approach is fundamentally, and intentionally, nonviolent. In *Welcoming Strangers*, we noted that violence is wrong because it always breaches at least one of the four principles explicated by Beauchamp and Childress. Violence causes harm, rarely does any good, does not respect the autonomy of the individual, and is often unfair. If we consider the other principles we discussed above—being faithful, respecting that which belongs to others, telling the truth, not being jealous of what others have, and moderation—it is clear here too that violence is fundamentally at odds with these moral principles. In other words, violence would be tested by these principles, and without very good reasons—that is higher order principles—violence ought to be morally rejected. Of greatest significance, among the principles we have suggested, for the well-being of children in care, are respect for others and what belongs to them, and nonviolence, refraining from harm.

Perhaps not surprisingly, when we have observed a mal-developed moral sense in the children we care for, it is the principles we have highlighted that are lacking. Parents and caregivers have not modeled respect, nonviolence, faithfulness, regard for what belongs to others, truth-telling, and contentment. In a too often chaotic, violent, and insecure environment, without good role models children easily pick up lack of respect, violence, and learn that to tell lies might well be the best way to stay out of trouble. With no other moral basis, these children in turn replicate their parents' behavior and the cycle of deprivation, neglect, violence and insecurity continues.

While parenting our birth children, and those foster children we had from babies, like most parents we engaged in a continual process of teaching and reinforcing the basic moral principles we considered above. A six-month-old may reach out of the pushchair to take something from a display in a store. Immediately, the parent responds, "No you can't have that, it is not yours." Or "Let's put it in the shopping cart as we have to pay for it before you can have it." Even though the baby may be pre-verbal, a moral sense is being developed. Most of this is just part of day-to-day parenting. It happens unconsciously. We doubt many parents think, "Now I am teaching moral sense."

As the babies grow, similar conversations take place. They happen in stores, in playgroups and at friends' houses. These children start to learn and understand that they can't just take something that is not theirs, or randomly hit other children. Sometimes these conversations involve tears and tantrums. Who hasn't experienced or observed those checkout tantrums over the candy placed at child level! The parent holds firm and moral sense is being developed—it is not acceptable to take something that belongs to someone else.

A common myth is that children in foster care are bad children. We reject the myth. But, it does present a dilemma for re-parents. Though we want to hold the children accountable for their actions, and in the process help them develop a moral sense, we don't want to consider them bad kids, or have others consider them bad kids. Such labels can stick with young people throughout their school years and even beyond. As with all children in foster care, the children and teenagers we have talked about have been victims of violence with the resulting trauma. Yet, how are we to view it when stealing, disrespect, or violence continue, and our attempts to develop a moral sense in the short term seem to fail? Is our child being willfully disobedience, or is their behavior a trauma based response? It is likely both, but we need to be aware and sensitive to the fact of abuse and trauma as mitigating circumstances. That does not mean we excuse the stealing, or ignore violent behavior. But it does help re-parents understand the behavior, and helps us resist the mindset that this child is simply a bad child. Loving, non-violent re-parenting is essential to help the child begin the process of healing from trauma, and in time to develop a healthy moral sense.

Sex and Morals

In *Welcoming Strangers*, we included a brief section about sexuality[24] where we talked about keeping teenagers safe from disease and, in the case of girls, pregnancy. We recognized that this was pragmatic, not ideal, as children as young as eleven and twelve have already had sexual partners. So here we want to look more closely at moral sense and sexuality.

Although we don't want to be gender stereotypical, in our experience the boys tend to feel it is macho to have sex with as many girls as they can. They are not shy to boast about their exploits, sometimes to the extent that we feel sure there is at least some exaggeration. While the girls can feel bullied or peer pressured to engage in sex before they really want to. Of course, we have, on occasion known girls actively to pursue boys and boys to feel peer pressured. Sex and morality is a difficult subject to address with any child. When a history of violence and abuse is added, it becomes even harder to do so. We both work in education so are not unaware of changing standards toward sex. In many ways it feels like the moral ground in regard to sexuality is changing.

*

Sallie was eight years old, or, as she liked to point out to us, nearly nine. With her blond curly hair and blue eyes, people often commented that she looked like a young Shirley Temple. Sallie was a chatterbox. She would talk about her day, her friends, and her life. Sometimes it felt like she talked non-stop. Sallie was one of those children, quite rare, who loved being in foster care. She was very vocal about it, telling anyone who would listen that we were her foster parents and she that loved us and our pugs. Today, she was quite excited. Sallie was driving with Jane from our home to the DSS building, a journey of about four miles. They were going to the monthly support group for foster and adoptive parents. The children were cared for in a different room and Sallie really enjoyed meeting her new friends there. As they drove Sallie was talking about what she had done at school that day. Jane was listening with half an ear while focusing on driving.

"Jane, do you know what I hate?"

"No what do you hate?" Jane responded quite expecting to hear about some unwelcome food item that had been part of her school lunch.

"I hate hearing people have sex," Sallie answered.

As Sallie continued her tale it became apparent that she had indeed been in close proximity to family members having sexual intercourse. As was her wont a couple of sentences later she changed topic and was chattering about something her teacher had said.

Sallie in many ways looked and acted a couple of years younger than her chronological age; she presented as a picture of innocence. Yet, here she was aware of and talking about sex as a norm in her world.

*

In *Welcoming Strangers*, we mentioned the shock when receiving our first placement to find the child's grandmother herself only in her early thirties was trapped in prostitution (we were very naive in those days).[25] Yet, that serves to illustrate the dilemma. Part of re-parenting is helping the child develop a moral sense around sexuality. However, as far as possible we don't want to condemn the choices their parents have made to the kids. That tends to cause divided loyalty and often ends in alienation of parents or re-parents.

One of the saddest things for us to watch is the lack of regard many of the teenagers have towards their own bodies. We talked about body image in more detail in regard to weight and size in Chapter 2. Here we simply want to note it as part of developing a moral strength, in terms of sexuality and cleanliness. Many of the teens feel worthless, they don't care about themselves.

We want to begin to develop a moral sense in all these areas that lead to a life of well-being. Our aim in developing this is to help the children and teenagers move towards healing from the violence of the past. We want them to graduate high school and go to university or enter the workforce. We want them prepared to make strong relationships and have fulfilled lives. To do this they will need to develop strong characters, overcoming early adversity is never easy. However, it is possible. We are still in contact with several of the young people who lived with us who are in stable relationships with children of their own. Their children are flourishing in their homes, the cycle has been broken.

Although we work hard at making sure we don't criticize the lifestyle of parents, there becomes a point, usually in late teens/early adulthood when the young person realizes that their parents are not living a healthy lifestyle.

*

We were walking at a local outdoor shopping precinct, when a shout stopped us, "Jane and Andy, it's ages since I saw you." Kaden came running up and gave us both a hug. Now a young man in his early twenties, Kaden had lived with us for several years. Throughout his early teenage years his dream, common with many kids in foster care, had been eventually to go home. He had seen no reason why he couldn't be with his parents. Even though they rarely had taken the opportunity to visit him, he had continued to make excuses for why they didn't turn up. Nor had they sent him birthday or Christmas presents, or even greetings. They were probably some of the more disinterested parents we have worked with.

After he had graduated high school and done a few semesters at a community college Kaden decided to return home. He was by this time old enough to discharge himself from foster care. Although we had encouraged him to keep in touch we hadn't seen him for the few months since his returning home.

"Kaden, lovely to see you. How are you doing? Are you still going to college and working at the same place?"

"I'm doing okay. I'm still working there and I've just moved out into my own place. I hated it with my parents."

"Oh, so sorry it didn't work out."

Kaden looked at us almost accusingly, "Why didn't you tell me they were losers? All they did was sit around all day drinking, smoking and watching TV. I was expected to pay all the bills. I had to give up college to earn extra money."

We spent longer talking with Kaden. We were very impressed. When Kaden had arrived on our doorstep he had looked downtrodden and underfed. The marks of fear, abuse and trauma were written all over him. He barely spoke, he ate little, was failing at school and showed no interest in anything. Gradually that changed sufficient enough that he was able to graduate from high school. Now before us stood the proof that the change was continuing. He had found the inner strength to leave family and all that signified behind. After a few minutes talking of his disillusionment with family, Kaden moved on to talking about his new apartment and his decision to get financial aid and return to college. We still keep in touch with Kaden and are happy to report that he continues to do well.

Final Things We Have Learned

1.

We recognized that moral sense began with us the carers. Not hypocritical. Walk the walk.

2.

We learned not to be judgmental, but provided guiding principles. Effectively, this means that we established clear boundaries for the household.

3.

We refused to punish moral failings, but rather used those failures as something to learn from.

4.

We learned that we needed to be ready to forgive mistakes and move on quickly, not dwelling on the mistake.

5.

We learned to have frequent and deliberate conversations about morality without using that word. As we watched movies, TV or saw the actions of friends we would comment on good things that were said and done. Conversely, we would discuss how certain actions harmed others.

6.

We learned to be quick with our praise when a child made a good decision. We would acknowledge how difficult a certain decision may have been and affirm their strength of character in choosing the right thing to do.

Notes

1 Cited in Aldous Huxley, *The Perennial Philosophy* (New York: Harper Collins, 1990), 178.
2 Paul Bloom, *Just Babies: The Origin of Good and Evil* (London: The Bodley Head, 2013), 18.

3 Charles Dickens, *The Christmas Books, Volume 1: A Christmas Carol/The Chimes* (Harmondsworth: Penguin Books, 1971), 96.
4 Steven Pinker, *The Better Angels of Our Nature: How Violence Has Declined* (New York: Viking, 2011), 622.
5 Steven Pinker, *The Blank Slate: The Modern Denial of Human Nature* (New York: Viking, 2002).
6 Ibid., 435–439.
7 Bloom, *Just Babies*, 8.
8 Ibid., 30.
9 Adam Smith, *The Wealth of Nations* (Harmondsworth: Penguin, 1970).
10 Adam Smith, *The Theory of Moral Sentiments* (Mineola: Dover, 2006), 3
11 Ibid., 4.
12 David Hume, *An Enquiry Concerning the Principles of Morals*, in *Moral Philosophy*, edited by Geoffrey Sayre-McCord (Indianapolis, IN: Hackett, 2006).
13 Ibid., 190.
14 David Hume, *A Treatise of Human Nature* (Harmondsworth: Penguin, 1969), 462.
15 Psalms 8:5.
16 Michael Puett and Christine Gross-Loh, *The Path: What Chinese Philosophers Can Teach Us About the Good Life* (New York: Simon & Schuster, 2016), 23ff.
17 Ibid., 44.
18 Ibid., 45.
19 Ibid., 53.
20 W. D. Ross, *The Right and the Good*, edited by Phillip Stratton-Lake (Oxford: Clarendon Press, 2002), 20.
21 Tom L. Beauchamp and James F. Childress, *Principles of Biomedical Ethics* (Oxford: Oxford University Press, 2009).
22 "The Ten Essential Precepts," http://sfzc.org/about-zen-center/principles-governance/ethics/ethical-principles/the-ten-essential-precepts, accessed September 6, 2018.
23 Steven Pinker, *Enlightenment Now: The Case for Reason, Science, Humanism, and Progress* (New York: Viking, 2018), 161–171.
24 Jane Hall Fitz-Gibbon and Andrew Fitz-Gibbon, *Welcoming Strangers: Nonviolent Re-parenting of Children in Foster Care* (Piscataway, NJ: Transaction, 2016).
25 Ibid., 5.

5 Nurturing Our Better Angel of Reason

In thinking about "the better angels of our nature," and using these psychological faculties as a lens through which to consider loving nonviolent re-parenting, we have followed the order used by Steven Pinker—empathy, self-control, moral sense, and reason. But, in truth we could have used any order, as the four faculties are intimately connected. In fact, we might make an argument for looking at reason first, for reason underlies, and strengthens, the other faculties. That reason underlies self-control and moral sense is obvious, even if moral sense is rooted in the capacity of benevolent sympathy. Yet, even empathy—most closely connected to feeling than thinking—requires a developed reasonable basis to develop adequately. Though everyone has the potential for empathy, we still need to develop it, and that requires a thoughtful response as to how. As with empathy, self-control and moral sense, we, as re-parents, need to demonstrate to our children that we are people who reason ourselves, and teach our children how to reason for themselves.

Readers will have noticed this interconnection of the four better angels through the stories we have used to illustrate these four areas. We have made somewhat hard separations for analytical purposes only. In young children and babies these faculties start to develop simultaneously, and continue to do so for many years as the brain grows and matures.

When parents engage in conversations with toddlers, they work on the better angels in turn, constantly teaching and reinforcing first one, then another:

> "Be gentle with that doggie, you don't want to hurt her." (Empathy)

> "I know you don't want to stop playing, but it is bedtime so let's put your toys away now." (Self-control)

> "Let's give your friend her toy back now. I can see you loved playing with it, but it belongs to her." (Moral sense)

> "Do you want to wear your red shirt or your blue shirt today?" (Reason)

In a similar way, when we re-parent children and teenagers, we help them develop these attributes as part of the daily task. In day-to-day re-parenting, we don't divide and separate empathy, self-control, moral sense, and reason, or even consciously focus on any of them specifically. Our stories often show the lack of these psychological attributes in the children we care for, but not in tidy categories. So, for example, the stories we have told of stealing illustrate a child who is short on empathy for others, or has little self-control, or undeveloped moral sense.

In this book, as in *Welcoming Strangers* before it, we have tried to help readers think about issues of violence and trauma, and to consider carefully how we might develop nonviolent responses. We have looked at why some children suffer trauma following violence, and why some ways of caring for these children are better than others. We have argued that further violence by carers—physically or emotionally—compounds the problem rather than helping to solve it. We have asked what kinds of strategies are best for an intentionally nonviolent care, and we have considered counter examples. In other words, in all of this we have made an appeal to reason. And for good reasons (pun intended)! Pinker makes the case that reason is a contra-indicator for violent behavior. That is, other things being equal, the more we apply reason, the less violent we are likely to be. We know the truth of this when someone becomes enraged, and is in danger of hurting themselves or someone else. A caring friend says, "Calm down! Be reasonable! Think about what you're doing!" The friend says such because reason is the opposite of impulsive, passion-filled, and often verbally or physically violent behavior. The parent who, in a fit of pique and frustration, lashes out at her child with hand, or handy implement, would likely not do it if she had time to think about it. After the initial rush of vindication at the child's cry of pain, it's likely that the mother is overtaken with feelings of guilt and shame, co-mingled with self-justification. "He had it coming!" "He deserved it!" He'd been working up to that all day!" But the small voice of reason quietly speaks, "He didn't really deserve it. He's frustrated too. His playing up masks his need for attention and love."

That inner voice of reason reflects a larger cultural shift that began in the modern period. Pinker argues that it was when people in Europe and America began to apply reason in a more systematic way, some five hundred years ago, that violence began to decline. The decline was slow, to be sure, but was steady and the long-term trend is that violence is still in decline. Common practices—public executions, cruelty to animals and children, routine torture of criminals, readily accepted pogroms and genocides—are now considered unreasonable. When we think about such violent practices, we search for a better way.

Perhaps strangely, given the good that has been achieved through it, reason, and its firstborn child reasonableness, are not always valued highly in contemporary society. Led by sometimes an impulsive media and, sadly, by political leaders who play to the crowd's baser instincts, many seem happier with gut feelings, intuition, and swift action. To pause, to become reflective, to think through difficult issues seems too ponderous, and as Pinker says, "Reason appears to have fallen on hard times."

Truth too, like reason, has seen better days. The two are intimately connected. Popular culture has imbibed a view that there is no such thing as truth. Each person, each party, each faction has its own "truth" and no one can judge between such truth claims. It is the confusion between the right to hold an opinion, or a belief, about something and the truth of such opinions. The situation is compounded in that prior political commitments influence the willingness to accept evidence-based truth. This confusion is seen in the widespread distrust of science. Sociologist Gordon Gauchat analyzed public acceptance of evidence-based policy and funding for science.[1] He began with an assumption that political persuasion would likely account for why some people distrusted science and why some accepted it. His findings were more complex. Some "lefties" mistrusted science when it came to nuclear power, while "righties" distrusted science with regard to climate change, thus confirming his hypothesis. However, the clearest factor in the mistrust of science, and its use in public policy, was conservative religious belief that considered evolution to be opposed to the Bible. Religious conservatives, who opposed evolution, tended to mistrust all science, and therefore opposed the use of evidence-based science as a basis for public policy. Of interest for our purposes, is that it was when religious dogma gradually gave way to reason from the beginnings of modernity, that violence began its steady decline (more on this below). The contemporary distrust of scientific reasoning, by a large minority in the United States, is part of the malaise of reason generally.

Philosophers have long considered truth to be justified beliefs. Much that we claim to be true is so because we can find good reasons for thinking it to be so. Truth claims are backed up by reasons. But, if it is true that all "truths" are equal, then the reasoning skills required to back up truth claims become redundant. Think what you will about anything at all, and such is true for you. The irony is, that if it is true that "all opinions are equally true," then it is equally true that "some opinions are false." This begs the question, and though it is a popular standpoint, most of do not accept the total relativity of truth claims. We have good reasons to think some things have more veracity (truthfulness) than others. Relativism with regard to truth makes the same fundamental mistakes as moral relativism. No one really acts as if it is true.

Despite the lack of trust in reason in popular culture, Pinker argues that "all things being equal, a smarter world is a less violent world."[2] Of course, irrationality and impulsiveness, with their associated violence, are part of the human lot and every culture in every age has its fair share. Yet, today's hard times for reason might well be a short term reaction to the slow and steady progress toward a more reasonable and less violent world. It might seem foolish to think so, but the long term trends favor reasonableness over violence.

However, much work remains to be done, and, though children are generally safer now than ever before, we still need the application of reason to the challenges of child care, to further reduce violence in the lives of children and their ensuing trauma. Reason along with empathy, self-control, and moral sense, is a foundation of loving nonviolent re-parenting. Reasonableness counters the often impulsive behavioral responses to children's acting out that often results in a screaming match, reckless punishment, and, all too frequently, a "good spanking."

Reasoning in the Foster Care System

In the foster care system, it is easy to see that reasonableness and good critical thinking skills are vital for the well-being of children. The system, at its best, makes decisions based on good reasons. Simplistically, when a child cannot live at home, they are taken into foster care. At a very basic level this may be true, but the reality is not so simple. Many people are involved in the decision making about the child. Reason is involved with every decision, and the process often begins long before the child reaches a foster placement. Reasoning underlies decision making such as:

- Is this child safe at home?
- Does he need to be removed from the birth home?
- Can relatives be found who would care for the child?
- And what foster home (of those available) will best meet her needs?

The overarching question ought always to be: "What is in the best interest of the child?" And to make those kinds of decisions good critical reasoning skills are essential. In terms of loving nonviolent re-parenting, that question is more precise in terms of what loving nonviolent care can provide to help the child recover from trauma induced by violence. Some options favored in the past—orphanages, residential centers that function as junior prisons, foster care based on outmoded and violent forms of discipline, boot camps—do not meet the needs of traumatized children.

Once a child is placed, a myriad of further decisions need to be reasoned out, and implemented: school and childcare, medical and dental, visitation, counseling, to mention but a few. Each of these requires a lot of thought and consideration. For example, the state sets a minimum requirement for visitation with birth families. However, there are still many decisions to be considered, such as whether a birth parent can have more visits than the minimum required by law. Certainly, this is advisable if the child is an infant and may ultimately return home, as bonding needs to happen with the birth family. Yet, this too brings questions to be carefully thought through.

As we were writing, Jane received a phone call from a new foster parent with a query. The carer had an infant who was probably returning home soon. Parental visits had been increased to every alternate day.

The foster carer was wondering if she should continue to provide diapers, bottles of baby milk, bibs, and changes of clothes for the baby. Her reasoning was that if the baby was returning home then the parents needed to take responsibility for these basic needs. Yet, she was concerned that the child may go hungry if she did not provide the milk. Jane had great sympathy with her. However, her advice could only be to talk to the caseworker and birth parents and make a reasonable plan with which all parties would be in agreement.

Where the visitation takes place also requires careful thought. It can be in the foster home, or in the family room at DSS, or even a safe space in the community. We have worked with birth parents in all these situations.

*

Many years ago we were fostering three young children: a brother and sister, both under four years old, and an unrelated seven-year-old boy. The birth mother of the youngest two was coming on a scheduled visit to our home. When we opened the door to welcome her in it was apparent she had been drinking. The smell of alcohol was strong, and she was a little unsteady. Jane called the caseworker to ask whether the visit should proceed. Talking it through, the caseworker and Jane decided that, due to the young ages of the children, and the mother showing no signs of violent behavior, the visit should proceed. However, the agreement was to terminate the visit at once if any aggression was shown, even calling the police if necessary. The caseworker also asked Jane not to mention that the mother was drunk in front of our other foster child, as she was unsure how it would affect him. In the end, the short visitation went well from the toddlers' viewpoint. Our seven-year-old seemed oblivious to her condition. But then, as the mother stumbled out of our driveway, the streetwise boy turned to us with a big grin and said, "It's a good job she didn't strike a match near her breathe we would have all exploded!" It is one of those fostering moments etched in our memories. Yet, that leads to another consideration for visits in the foster home.

*

We have had many parents visit in our home, especially if the child is soon to return home. However, on several occasions, parents eagerly expected by their children did not arrive. Tender children are further traumatized in their perceived further rejection. If the parents do attend visitation, time to leave can be very upsetting, with young children often in tears. It is difficult for everyone concerned. Our preference has been that visits take place at the DSS building with transportation provided by the caseworker or case aide when possible, at least in the early days of a placement. This can still be traumatic for the children especially if the separation from the birth parents is still raw. When it is time to say goodbye to their parents, the children can be re-traumatized, as separation from their parents is re-enacted. This is the main reason we prefer DSS workers to transport. It is healthier for the children if we are not involved in that re-enactment, but simply there to welcome the children home.

Who supervises a visit, and who should attend, also requires careful thought.

*

We had the older half of a large sibling group placed with us. The remaining younger children were placed with another foster family with whom we were friends. It was a good arrangement, as between us we could ensure all the siblings stayed in touch with frequent visits and even occasional outings together. The birth parent had asked if the visitation could be in the park. It was summer, and the weather was perfect for an outdoor visitation. As it was a weekend, the caseworker asked if it could be supervised by ourselves or the other family. It was more difficult for us as we had other children placed in our home at the time. Our friend Helen offered to take them all and supervise the visit. Two hours later, she returned to our home. She looked exhausted! In her words, the visit had been chaotic. The parents had brought other friends and relatives including many additional children, all of whom had run around wildly together with our children. Helen was very concerned. With such a large number of children, and adults, she hadn't felt she could adequately supervise. It was a long way from the expected quiet visit in the park with the birth mother and father. Although, on return home, our kids said it had been fun to see friends and relatives, but by the next day they were complaining that they hadn't really talked to their parents. Conversations with the caseworker resulted in the birth-parents being advised that visitation should be only between themselves and the children. If any other relatives would like to see the children, then separate arrangements could be made for them.

*

As well as these day-to-day decisions, consideration must be made about the child's future. Of course, ultimately, it is not a re-parent who makes this decision but the court in conjunction with input from DSS, caseworkers, and lawyers. However, the re-parent is the one who is involved with the children on a daily basis and may have some valuable insights to share.

Sometimes the re-parent and the caseworker may not agree about what is in the best interest of the child. That is hard and needs lots of conversation and reasoning on both parts as decisions are made. However, it is definitely in the child's best interest for everyone involved to be working towards the same goal. Ultimately, foster carers may have to remind themselves that these are not "their" children to make decisions for, but those for whom they are caring, for as long as they need a home. Re-parents are also the ones who must explain court and DSS decisions to the children and help them come to terms with them. It can be difficult to help a child understand why they only get to see their parent once a week. Conversations explaining the situation will need to be frequently re-visited to help a child, or even a teenager, grasp the situation.

*

Karen had been having supervised visitation for many months. It was decided that the next step in trying to get reunification with her mother (a single parent) was to allow unsupervised visits. Not only would she be alone with her mother for the first time in many months, but the visits were scheduled to be at her parent's apartment. We were concerned; Karen was only ten and had some developmental delays due to fetal alcohol syndrome. Jane asked Karen whether she felt safe going home. "Oh yes," she replied cheerfully, "I'll check the bins on the way in. If there are a lot of bottles [alcohol] I'll make sure there is always a door behind me." Although certainly a far from ideal situation, Karen had learned to reason enough to keep herself safe.

*

Marina was several years older than Karen. She also had been raised by a single parent who struggled with alcoholism. Marina struggled with the erratic behavior of her mother. She questioned why she behaved as she did, and was often embarrassed by and angry with her mother. We tried to help Marina understand about alcoholism as we wanted her to maintain that relationship even though returning home was unlikely. Marina tried hard to understand for several months. Then one day, she came to us and said, "My mom's ill, isn't she?" By reasoning that her mother's alcoholism was a sickness, Marina was able to accept that her mother loved her but couldn't care for her. She reasoned that the neglect she had suffered in the past wasn't because she wasn't liked but because mom was sick. It was a major turning point for Marina.

*

Another area we have had to help children accept is when a parent is incarcerated. Sadly, having a parent in prison is the norm for many families. Nevertheless, it can be a hard adjustment for any child.

*

Lewis lived with us for nearly three years as a young teenager. In all that time he never mentioned his father was in prison. In fact, he never mentioned his father. He had no contact with him, nor did he want any. There were no letters, no phone calls, no birthday cards. Lewis showed no emotion regarding his father, it was as if he didn't exist.

*

Ray was just the opposite extreme. He talked about his father on a daily basis. He longed to be with him. He counted the weeks until he would be released from jail. Some of his ideas about dad getting a big house, a job, and him moving in the same day he was released, were unrealistic.

We tried to prepare him. We explained that the housing project where his dad would live for the first few months after release was not a suitable place for Ray to live. We talked about the need to get to know his father again. We explained that he would stay with us for a little while longer but with lots of visits to his dad. Even though Ray was fourteen, he was unable to understand the reasoning that it needed to be done in this way, both for his safety and logistical reasons. Ray found any form of reasoning hard, it was a skill he had never learned. All he could say was that when dad came home he was going to go and live with him. His adjustment to the reality was hard. In the first few weeks after his parent was released Travis regressed in several areas. Although the plan, agreed and supported by everyone, was that he would return home in the near future. He could not grasp the reasons why it wasn't immediate, even with the simple fact that an apartment needed to be found. His violent behavior escalated both at home and school to such an extent that he was moved to a residential setting. For re-parents that is always a sad time, mixed with a little guilt that we hadn't been able to do more. We always talk it through and wonder if there was anything we could have done differently. Ultimately our conviction remains that the best way to help these young victims of violence is with intentional loving nonviolence.

*

Kim and Harper were younger. They were our first experience of taking children to visit a parent in jail, who they would see every two weeks. Prior to the first visit we tried to help them understand a little about why they would not be able to hug their father or sit on his knee. Jane took them along with their caseworker. Two adults were necessary as the young children were a few years apart in age. The arrangements were that the children could request to leave when they needed to. It was anticipated that little Kim would not be able to manage the whole time, so the plan was that Jane would take her home when necessary leaving the caseworker to bring Harper along later. A jail visit is traumatic for any child. After a few minutes in the waiting room we were escorted to the imposing steel door. The four of us went through, and the door locked behind us. This left us in a small space with a locked door behind and in front of us. Jane felt a momentary flash of panic before reason took over and she was able to reassure the children that this was normal procedure. A voice over a speaker instructed us to place any bags, phones or other belongings in the locker to our side. Thankfully, we had enquired before the visit about whether the children could bring little gifts for their father. We had been told that was not allowed although things could be mailed for him, so there was no disappointment in leaving things behind that were planned as gifts. The door in front of us then opened and we were led to the visiting room. The caseworker, children and I sat at a desk on one side of a large Plexiglas screen. Their father sat on the other side. Kim and Harper were able to talk freely to their father. The Plexiglas didn't go all the way to the ceiling and no one objected when the children stood on the desk and were able touch their father over the top. As anticipated Kim grew restless before the time allocated, and Jane took her out with her father's approval after they had said their goodbyes. It is hard to help a child reason many things about such visit—the lack of contact, nothing to play with or draw on, the scary experience of being between two doors and the reality that dad had to stay there. Though in today's polarized political climate, the police often receive a bad press, every police officer, sheriff's deputy, and state trooper who were present during these times have been great. Without exception, the children have been treated kindly and respectfully. We are sure that went some way to lessening the trauma of such visits.

Teens Again

In the latter years of our foster career, as we took older children, almost all of our children have had a mental health diagnosis. Whether our experience reflects an increasing problem, or a greater awareness of mental health issues is unclear to us. Behaviors and problems that we encountered in the early years of our fostering career were simply attributed to trauma, violence, and a poor social background. Now, a diagnosis is sought for these same problems. Increasingly children are being diagnosed with serious mental health problems at a much younger age.

*

Our first teenager with a mental health diagnosis was seventeen-year-old Jana. We were asked if we could take her for about a month as she was being discharged from a psychiatric hospital, and a place had been obtained for her at a supervised independent living facility. However, at the time of her discharge they were full and did not anticipate having space for her for at least three weeks. Hence the need for a bridging placement in foster care.

Jana arrived nervously but settled well. She seemed younger than her age and related well to the other children in the household. She bore the deep scars of her recent suicide attempt; scars that were both physical and mental. Due to the short duration of the placement we did not receive much information about her background. We knew only that she had been adopted several years earlier. The adoptive placement had broken down, with no further contact with the family. We were not told why the adoption had broken down. However, it had resulted in a deep depression, leading to her very serious suicide attempt. The hospital stay had helped her. Jana talked to us about her future hopes and career plans.

*

Sadly, since that first placement of a teenager who had attempted, or threatened, to commit suicide we have had several more. They have mainly, although not exclusively, been girls. The Centers for Disease Control and Prevention (CDC) comment, "Suicide is the third leading cause of death for youth between the ages of 10 and 24, and results in approximately 4,600 lives lost each year."[3] In our county, if a child in foster care is self-harming or threatening suicide it is mandated to take them for a psychological examination. Jane has spent several nights in the ER of our local hospital with young people who have to be assessed following threats of self-harm. Of our children, only two have been admitted the others have all returned home with us. The CDC report on this serious issue stated, "Each year, approximately 157,000 youth between the ages of 10 and 24 are treated in Emergency Departments across the U.S. for self-inflicted injuries."[4]

Our experience of taking more females to the hospital is borne out by the data that show that more girls disclose suicide ideation and self-harm. However, the data also show that more boys actually do commit suicide. A comparison of youth who made a serious suicide attempt showed that the death rate was 81.7 percent male *vs* 45.6 percent female.[5] This disparity has been termed the "gender paradox,"[6] and is a cause for concern for re-parents.

*

Terry came to us with a diagnosis of Asperger's (now subsumed under autism spectrum disorder). He had many of the typical attributes of what is known colloquially as an "Aspie kid." He was forever pacing around the house. Even if he was watching television with us he would stand behind the sofa pacing backward and forward rather than sitting with us. He would only eat certain foods. After he had been with us for four months, we decided to take him out to a restaurant. We knew this would be hard for him, but we were trying to encourage him to have more outings. We chose a breakfast, thinking that would be easier for him, and framed it as a special Christmas Eve treat.

He agreed to try the restaurant, so we took him and the other two children in the household at the time. He looked at the menu, shunned all the suggested breakfast platters and insisted on only one food item. We asked if we could have a plate of only hash browns! Even posing that question to the waitress had proved too much for Terry. He slid off his chair and onto the floor under the table. Once the food was delivered he put his hand up every few seconds to get another hash brown off his plate! Happily, no one in the restaurant commented about his behavior. We were able to ignore him sitting on the floor, so he could enjoy his first restaurant experience at his own comfort level. Terry was delighted with the trip. He had enjoyed it and wanted to go again soon. Terry was with us several years and gradually became more comfortable in many different social situations. By the time he left us he would happily go to any restaurant—the local Mexican restaurant was his favorite—and behave appropriately.

At school, Terry kept his head down on his desk, refusing to participate verbally in any lesson. However, it became clear that he was learning a lot.

Although he barely spoke at school he would tell us about characters in books the class had read. We advocated for him, suggesting his teachers did not specifically interact with him until he was comfortable in their presence. When the school installed hallway cameras, Terry became very unsettled as he did not like his picture taken. Yet, by that time, he had made significant progress in learning to reason. If he didn't want his picture taken he must avoid the cameras. Indeed, he learned where all the cameras were placed and then mapped out routes between his various classes and the dining hall. These were not always the shortest routes, but anything was preferable to being seen on camera. And he still managed to get to the dining hall as one of the first students to arrive for lunch, thus avoiding his peers. He would collect his meal and return to his special education classroom where arrangements had been made for him to eat lunch. Terry spent five years at high school and was ultimately able to walk with his graduating class. A very big achievement for him.

*

It can be especially difficult to help teenagers and children with any of these issues to reason. In Chapter 1 we told the story of Juanita, who frequently refused her psychiatric medication. He could not hear the reasoning that he was able to do better at school, in the home and community as he was less violent when he took it. Helping teenagers to learn reason is not an easy task, nor is it a quick one. It needs consistent re-parenting. Juanita was still struggling to understand why she should take her medication when she left our care. They were both with us for about a year, and still had much to learn as they continue their journey towards adulthood.

Patriarchy

It is sometimes said that we live in a post-feminist world; that equality has been achieved, and that women now have all the same privileges as men. Our experience in foster care suggests otherwise. The dismissive attitude toward females by most of the boys we have cared for—superiority, nonchalance, belittling, mocking, domination—is pervasive. Many of the teenage boys we have cared for have already imbibed the idea of male entitlement. We have tried, through example and careful explanation, to help these boys, and young adults, re-think their view of women. We challenge the patriarchal viewpoint, though it is often deeply ingrained, even in young boys. We have realized that we are wading against a strong current pervasive in our culture from the music the kids listen to, to the movies they watch, to the actions and expressions of politicians. Men can have their cake and eat it! And these boys know it.

In the story of Jaquan and Jacinda (Chapter 3) we talked about how Jaquan had already become a patriarch. He made all the decisions, and Jacinda wasn't even allowed to make her own choice about what she wore, or what she ate. If asked a question, she would look to Jaquan before answering, a fearful look in her eyes if she said something wrong. Though this was an extreme case, we have faced patriarchy in the children we care for many times. Many of these teenagers have come from a culture that is patriarchal, as well as homophobic and racist. Women are seen merely to serve men. Sometimes the conversations we have had with boys have left us fearful that they will eventually be involved in domestic violence. Their attitude seems to be that women need to be kept in their place, and if violence is needed to achieve that, so be it. In 2014, the United Nations Children's Fund (UNICEF) produced a report entitled *Hidden in Plain Sight*. Their research confirms that patriarchy is still rampant. Here are just three of the many facts included in their literature:

- Close to half of all girls aged fifteen to nineteen worldwide (around 126 million) think a husband is sometimes justified in hitting or beating his wife.
- One in three adolescent girls aged fifteen to nineteen worldwide (84 million) have been victims of any emotional, physical or sexual violence committed by their husbands or partners at some point in their lives.
- Around 120 million girls under the age of twenty (about one in ten) have been subjected to forced sexual intercourse or other forced sexual acts at some point in their lives.[7]

As nonviolent re-parents important conversations about women's roles in society need to happen with both boys and girls. In many cases it will be remedial work trying to change how teenagers think about the subject. As with the other psychological attributes we have considered, how to think will need to be addressed many times. Often it will be in small bites. Re-parents will use all opportunities to drop a hint here and there.

Of course, it is not just conversation with teenagers. We start talking about these things as early as possible to try to help each child view the opposite gender in a non-stereotypical way.

Nigerian feminist Chimamanda Ngozi Adiche addresses this:

We do a great disservice to boys in how we raise them. We stifle the humanity of boys. We define masculinity in a *very* narrow way. Masculinity is a hard, small cage, and we put boys inside this cage. We teach boys to be afraid of fear, of weakness, of vulnerability . . . And then we do a much greater disservice to girls, because we raise them to cater to the fragile egos of males. We teach girls to shrink themselves, to make themselves smaller.[8]

Creating Memories . . . Birthdays and Holidays

One of the ways to help children develop reason is by helping them make sense of their lives: the way they think about themselves, others and the world they live in. Part of this is marking the years through special events and occasions. It helps to create a narrative framework for their lives. When our children were small one of the phrases often heard in our house was "do you remember," followed by a tale of a previous event or trip. Often it was little things that triggered these memories; a photo, or a trip or a scene in a movie.

With hindsight, we realize that we have helped to create memories for our children, and often without forethought. We would initiate conversations which would include reference to past events. We would be driving and say things like, "Do you remember when we climbed that hill?" Or, "Do you remember we stopped there for lunch when we were going on the holiday to Portsmouth?"

Or we could be watching television and comment on a place we had visited or we could re-visit a (British) National Trust property and comment on what we had enjoyed on our last trip there. Conversations always flowed after comments like these. Of course, at that time we had no idea we were creating memories. We were just doing what good parents have always done: conversing with their children. It was only later, as we started to meet children who had few memories of their childhood, that we started to realize the significance of these early conversations. Each time we say, "do you remember?" it reinforced the event. It keeps the memory alive. It builds history into childhood.

One day, as a young teenager, our eldest son said, "I remember my great-grandfather. I remember him holding me under the Christmas Tree." Jane's grandfather died just after our eldest son turned one year old. We are fairly convinced that this memory was in part created because of a lovely photo we have in one of our albums (pre-digital). At the time the photograph was taken our son was just ten weeks old. He is wearing a bright yellow outfit and lying very contently in the arms of his great-grandfather gazing up into his face. As our son stated they sat in an armchair with the Christmas tree towering above them. The early photograph, viewed often in his childhood, helped our son create the narrative of his life. It is certainly a "true" memory, but a memory established through remembrance and conversation. Did our son suddenly have a flashback to being ten weeks old? We doubt it. More likely, each time the children looked through the photograph albums we talked about it. We re-enforced the time, the occasion, the information about his great-grandfather, and so the memory was kept alive.

As we were writing this chapter a message just arrived from our other son. He and our daughter-in-law had taken their three children for a weekend in the city where the eldest two girls were born. In his text, he wrote about how he wanted the girls to see where they had been born and spent their early years. Stability and a sense of place is important as children mature. It gives them a firm foundation, and develops a sense of belonging.

We have helped many children re-create their own history. These histories—narratives of their lives—are often far from complete, but do give a sense of past. In the days of pre-digital photography, we did this through

"Life Books," which are scrapbooks that move with the child from their foster placement to their next home. The "Life Book" contains their own history. Often the children are engaged in this process and it helps them develop reason. Sometimes photographs can be obtained from birth parents, but not always.

*

Ellie and Ethan, a young sister and brother, came to us when they were six and nine years old with very little sense of their history. To create a sense of identity for them with the help of the caseworker we found out where they had been born, and started with a picture of the hospital announcing their birth details. It was only a little thing to do, but was significant for the children, and it gave them a beginning. We also uncovered information about their previous schools and included that in their "Life Books.". Ellie and Ethan drew pictures of their home and their family and friends especially for their book. Having tried to create a sense of history it was important to include the date they moved to our house. Then it was easy to do, by including photographs of all the places we visited with them over the next two years. We also added schools and teachers' names, vacations, birthday cards, parties and lists of gifts.

Reasoning Nonviolently

Reason—the way we think about ourselves, others and the world in which we live—is what we termed, in *Welcoming Strangers*, the reflective function in our understanding of nonviolent practice. As we reason about violence, nonviolence and children, we internalize the principles of nonviolence. In this way, reason interacts with the ways we feel, as we are conscientized to the violence children still suffer, and with our ability to make nonviolent choices as we intentionalize nonviolence as a way of life. This interaction is illustrated in Figure 5.1.

Reason is thus an important component in reducing violence for children in foster care. From our experience, we need to take care in three areas with regard to the acceptance of violence, where reason is too often overshadowed: culture and tradition, religious dogma, and peer pressure.

To be sure our culture is enamored of violence, and we are still smitten with the idea that violence always works as a last resort. In other words, though we may try nonviolent means, if all else fails violence will work things out. More than any other area this applies to the care of children. Our cultural tradition tells us that violence, hitting, and hurting children will change their behavior. Reason challenges this thinking, and we made our case for this in *Welcoming Strangers*. But, to challenge such a deeply held tradition requires persistence and courage. Simply because something is generally accepted, does not mean it passes the test of reason. We have good reasons to say that violence on children does not produce the effects claimed.

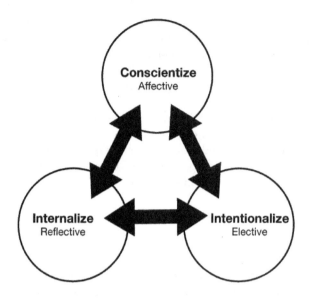

Figure 5.1 Nonviolent Practice.

Violence against children in the home is often a function of religious beliefs that suggest the biblical approach to childrearing is "spare the rod and spoil the child." In our training courses on nonviolent re-parenting we have found it necessary to tackle head-on the approach that says the Bible understood in this way is opposed to the reasonable and nonviolent care of children. Some religious parents struggle with a sense of disloyalty, or even disobedience to God, if they disregard what they think is a biblical injunction. The juxtaposition "the Bible says" and "reason suggests" is a difficult one for religious conservatives to manage. Our approach is to try to help such people understand that there are many approaches to religious faith and understandings of the Bible. Some principles in the Bible, such as those relating to childcare, are as historically conditioned and irrelevant today as the notion of a domed firmament with holes for the rain. We point to universal principles in sacred scripture such as compassion and kindness, and reason that such an approach tends toward greater well-being than a legalistic reading of the Bible. Many caring parents make the move, but some still struggle to square the circle of their religious beliefs and reason.

In *Welcoming Strangers*, we looked at the influence of religion in the early modern period with its understanding that childrearing was a matter of breaking a child's will. Under the influence of religious dogma that viewed children as sinful and wayward from birth, the parental task was—like a young wild horse—to break the child's will. This was accomplished as often than not through violence. Though the dogma is not influential today, many still perceive their parental task to be a contest of wills. Is the child's will stronger than the parents? Who will break first in the contest? Who has the ultimate control? Reason comes to our aid in reframing the parental task from the contest between adult and child into thinking through how best to help both parent and child control their baser instincts and impulses, and provide a framework for the nonviolent well-being of all. Pinker says, "Reason can also be a force against violence when it abstracts violence itself as a mental category and constructs it as a problem to be solved rather than a contest to win."[9]

Peer pressure, too, often works against reason. If your family and friends use violence on children as a means of control, why shouldn't you? What will they think if you are "soft" with your children? To follow the dictates of reason against pressure from one's peers is a tough, but necessary call for the well-being and healing of children in our care.

Final things we have learned

1.

Become a better re-parent by reading books (like this one) and watching competent documentaries, attending training courses and, most importantly, thinking through the information you receive. That is, don't simply accept information at face value. Rather, wrestle with it, critique it, compare it with experience and what you have learned elsewhere. And be willing to change your mind as more compelling arguments are presented. In other words, become a more educated, more aware, and more engaged carer.

2.

Translate what you learn into practice with the children you care for, both in terms of your personal caring, but also in nurturing children to reason for themselves.

3.

Give choices to the children you care for to help develop reasoning skills. As we demonstrated in *Welcoming Strangers*, many children who come into foster care are unable to make choices. Questions like "What would you like for breakfast?" or "What do you want to wear?" tend to leave some children paralyzed, unable to give an answer. From experience, initially, choices need to be limited to only two items:

"Do you want peanut butter or cream cheese on your bagel?"

"Do you want to wear the red shirt or the blue shirt today?"

The process is helped when the items offered are physically shown to the child. As the reasoning skills become more developed the choices can become more complex. Do you want peanut butter or cream cheese on your bagel, or would you prefer cereal? What color shirt would you like to wear today?

4.

Make each child feel valued for their ideas and suggestions. Their choices should be affirmed even when different than those we would make.

*

Bella had just started to choose her own clothes each day. This showed much progress from the little girl who had been unable to make any decision. She would often choose clothes that didn't really match, or materials that might prove a little unsuitable for the day. Other than ask her if she was sure she wouldn't be too cold or too hot we applauded her decisions (extra sweaters could always be added to school backpacks to ensure her comfort).

5.

Create examples for the child to see and hear. As adults we use reasoning skills all the time, mostly unconsciously. Start to speak aloud your reasoning on a situation, showing your thought process. If I do that, this will happen, or if I do that this will happen:

> "If I buy this big box of cereal, it works out cheaper but it may go bad before we eat it all. Therefore, I might not save money on it in the long run."

> "The weather forecast says it may rain and be windy today. I wonder if it would be sensible to take my umbrella, or I wonder if the wind will be too strong for the umbrella and blow it away?"

6.

Help children work through solving their own problems. Don't always work it out for them.

7.

Help young people identify how they are feeling. Discuss their feelings with them and validate them. When teenagers and children are having bad moments, when asked how they feel they will often say that they are "mad" or "sad." In trying to get them to understand why they are feeling "mad" or "sad" we can find new ways to help them to express their more nuanced feelings.

*

The caseworker dropped Mark back at our home. He had been on a scheduled visit with his birth family in the family room at DSS. The early return and the look on Mark's face showed it had not gone well. Mark ran upstairs to his bedroom, kicking walls and banging doors en route. The caseworker hurriedly shared that the family had not turned up. Mark was understandably upset. We were left with what is always a hard task for a foster carer: consoling a child who had anticipated seeing his family that day. Part of that task is to help Mark to understand his feelings.

When we talked to him all he could say was, "I'm mad." This wasn't directed specifically at anyone, just the only way he could verbalize what was happening to him emotionally. Careful conversation, after a time of quiet, helped him to examine his feelings a little more and reason why he felt that way: disappointed because he had looked forward to the visit; rejected because he felt his family didn't care; sad because he loved his mother; scared because they may not want him anymore; worried in case they were ill or dead. Helping Mark identify his feelings didn't change the situation. However, it did help to move him out of the basic, "I'm mad." We were able to show him that as he began to reason out why he felt the way he did, we could begin to address some of his worries. With Mark we were able to call the caseworker asking her to check the family was physically okay. We talked to Mark in an age-appropriate way to express his sadness, and to realize that his family had not rejected him, but rather that events had overtaken them.

8.

Help teenagers set goals and challenges and work toward them.

9.

Think about consequences: natural, foreseeable, and, through dialogue, agreed upon.

10.

Ask open-ended questions to help children develop their own reasoning skills.

Notes

1 Gordon Gauchat, "The Political Context of Science in the United States: Public Acceptance of Evidence-Based Policy and Science Funding," *Social Forces*, vol. 94, no. 2 (December 2015), 723–746.
2 Steven Pinker, *The Better Angels of Our Nature: How Violence Has Declined* (New York: Viking, 2011), 642.

3 Centers for Disease Control and Prevention, "Suicide Among Youth," 2017, www.cdc.gov/healthcommunication/toolstemplates/entertainmented/tips/SuicideYouth.html, accessed May 17, 2018.

4 Ibid.

5 Anne Rhodes et al, "Antecedents and sex/gender differences in youth suicidal behaviour". World Journal of Psychiatry, vol. 4, no. 4 (December 14, 2014), 120–132, www.ncbi.nlm.nih.gov/pmc/articles/PMC4274584, accessed May 18, 2018.

6 Ibid.

7 United Nations Children's Fund, *Hidden in Plain Sight: A Statistical Analysis of Violence against Children* (New York: UNICEF, 2014), 202.

8 Chimamanda Ngozi Adiche, *We Should all be Feminists* (New York: Anchor Books, 2012), 26–27.

9 Ibid., 646.

Postscript

In both *Welcoming Strangers* and *Nurturing Strangers*, we have challenged conventional thinking about violence, and the use of violence in changing children's behavior. We have looked especially at the use of violence in the foster care system. Our observation is that every child in care has been a victim of violence in one or several ways—physical, emotional, sexual, and systemic. Though some children seem to weather the storm of their early childhood, many suffer trauma as a result of their chaotic and violent start to life. It is all too easy to continue with the old conventional wisdom that violence is the most effective way to solve problems—especially problems with children. Further violence in the system only compounds the problem. We have suggested that to help these children heal from their violence induced trauma requires a loving, intentionally nonviolent home, with carers who have internalized and practice nonviolence.

To become such a carer requires a great deal of inner work, where, through habituation, the carer comes to terms with their own inner violence and tendency to hurt others. The carer develops, too, the character traits essential to becoming a nonviolent person. Such work requires patience and perseverance, and is a long term process.

We have shared our experience of re-parenting traumatized children and teenagers—our successes and failures—as we have built a nonviolent home. We started fostering in our twenties when our two oldest birth children were little more than toddlers. We only had a desire to try to help other little ones who needed a home. Often, as we entered new and uncharted waters with a child we felt we were fumbling for the best way to handle the situation. We never expected to be writing about things we had learned in a foster care journey that spanned 35 years. Our books are written both from our experience in caring, and from a strong foundation in education, in philosophy, and in the social sciences.

In this book, we have looked at an overall strategy for becoming nonviolent through the lens of what psychologist Steven Pinker terms the better angels of our nature—empathy, self-control, moral sense, and reason. Deliberately habituating these psychological faculties, and helping our children do the same is the best long term strategy we can imagine.

Throughout our journey, in common with many foster parents, many times we have looked back and wished we had done or said something differently.

Nonetheless, despite the hurdles and challenges, our conviction remains that the intentional use of nonviolence is the best way to counteract the violence that the children we care for have experienced. We have never wished that we had chosen a more violent way.

Our hope is that more carers, caseworkers, and case managers will adopt intentional nonviolence as a way of helping children heal from their trauma. We hope, too, that many new foster carers will take up the mantle and continue this vital work.

*

At the time of writing, we have been without children for over a year. Our time has been given to teaching and training others. Our last two teenagers had left us the previous summer. In the emotional roller coaster that is foster caring, one successfully returned home to his birth family after three years with us, the other, after a few short weeks in our home, went to an institution to receive further help overcoming his recreational drug usage.

*

Jane was returning home after a long and busy day. She heard the ping indicating a text had arrived. As she parked in the driveway she saw it was a text from Shona, who had left us for independent living some three years before. We had not seen her since, but had received the very occasional text from her. This one was came as a big surprise.

The ensuing text conversation read:

- Jane, can you run me to the hospital?
- Why what's up?
- I've been leaking for a couple days and my back feels like it's on fire. I think I'm starting labor.
- We'll be there.
- Can you take my boyfriend too? And can you let me have some money?

After a long, hard day, an unexpected trip to the emergency room was the last thing we wanted to do. Nevertheless, we were both very fond of Shona and wanted to help if possible. We rushed some food and set off to the address she had given us. After hugs all round, a very pregnant teenager plus her boyfriend climbed into our car. It was strange, as we chatted together on the drive to the emergency room. The three years since our last meeting seemed to disappear, and it felt like she had never left our care. She even asked us how it felt to be soon foster grandparents.

At the hospital, we remained with her throughout the booking-in process and helped her settle in her room. Then with another hug we left the young couple together to prepare to welcome their child with instructions to text if anything further was needed.

We wait . . .

Bibliography

Adiche, Chimamanda Ngozi. *We Should All Be Feminists*. New York: Anchor Books, 2012.

Ainslie, George. "Hyperbolic Discounting." In *Choice Over Time*, edited by George Lowenstein and Jon Elster. New York: Russell Sage Publications, 1992.

———. "Hyperbolic Discounting as a Factor in Addiction: A Critical Analysis." In *Choice, Behavioral Economics and Addiction*, edited by Rudy E. Vuchinich and Nick Heather. Boston, MA: Pergamon, 2003.

Ashley, Lawrence. "Guest Foreword." In *Thinking About Addiction: Hyperbolic Discounting and Responsible Agency*, written by Craig Hanson. Amsterdam: Rodopi, 2006.

Beauchamp, Tom L., and James F. Childress. *Principles of Biomedical Ethic*. Oxford: Oxford University Press, 2009.

Berger, Peter, and Thomas Luckmann. *The Social Construction of Reality: A Treatise in the Sociology of Knowledge*. New York: Anchor, 1967.

Blackburn, Simon. *Think*. Oxford: Oxford University Press, 1999.

Bloom, Paul. *Just Babies: The Origin of Good and Evil*. London: The Bodley Head, 2013.

Centers for Disease Control and Prevention. "About the CDC–Kaiser ACE Study." www.cdc.gov/violenceprevention/acestudy/about.html. Accessed September 10, 2018.

———. "Suicide among Youth." 2017. www.cdc.gov/healthcommunication/toolstemplates/entertainmented/tips/SuicideYouth.html. Accessed May 17, 2018.

Child Trends Data Bank. *Attitudes Toward Spanking*. Bethesda: Child Trends, 2015.

Child Welfare Information Gateway. "Sibling Issues in Foster Care." January 2013. www.childwelfare.gov/pubpdfs/siblingissues.pdf. Accessed April 2, 2018.

Clausen, June M., John Landsverk, William Granger, David Chadwick and Alan Litrownik. "Medical Health Problems of Children in Foster Care." *Journal of Child and Family Studies*, vol. 7, no. 3 (1998), 283–296. www.researchgate.net/profile/Alan_Litrownik/publication/226139536_Mental_Health_Problems_of_Children_in_Foster_Care/links/56e34da408ae68afa10ca98f/Mental-Health-Problems-of-Children-in-Foster-Care.pdf. Accessed May 2, 2018.

Congress.gov. "Fostering Connections to Success and Increasing Adoptions Act of 2008." www.congress.gov/bill/110th-congress/house-bill/6893. Accessed April 2, 2008.

De Waal, Frans. *The Age of Empathy: Nature's Lessons for a Kinder Society*. New York: Three Rivers Press, 2009.

Descartes, René. *Discourse on Method and Meditations on First Philosophy*. Translated by Donald A. Cress. Indianapolis, IN: Hackett, 1998.

Fields, Karen E., and Barbara J. Fields. *Racecraft: The Soul of Inequality in American Life*. New York: Versa, 2012.

Fitz-Gibbon, Andrew. "Today I Am Black Too, or Why Racism is Unsustainable." *The Abbot's Blog*. June 21, 2015. https://lindisfarnecommunity.blogspot.com/2015/06/today-i-black-too-or-why-racism-is.html. Accessed September 6, 2018.

Fitz-Gibbon, Jane Hall, and Andrew Fitz-Gibbon. *Welcoming Strangers: Nonviolent Re-parenting of Children in Foster Care*. Piscataway, NJ: Transaction, 2016.

Gauchat, Gordon. "The Political Context of Science in the United States: Public Acceptance of Evidence-Based Policy and Science Funding." *Social Forces*, vol. 94, no. 2 (December 2015), 723–746.

Greiner, Rae. "1909: The Introduction of the Word 'Empathy' into English." In *BRANCH: Britain, Representation and Nineteenth-Century History*, edited by Dino Franco Felluga. Extension of Romanticism and Victorianism on the Net. www.branchcollective.org/?ps_articles=rae-greiner-1909-the-introduction-of-the-word-empathy-into-english. Accessed March 12, 2018.

Hanson, Craig. *Thinking about Addiction: Hyperbolic Discounting and Responsible Agency*. Amsterdam: Rodopi, 2006.

Hume, David. "An Enquiry Concerning the Principles of Morals." In *Moral Philosophy*, edited by Geoffrey Sayre-McCord. Indianapolis, IN: Hackett, 2006.

———. *A Treatise of Human Nature*. London: Penguin, 1969.

Huxley Aldous. *The Perennial Philosophy*. New York: HarperCollins, 1990.

Koepp, M. J., R. N. Gunn, A. D. Lawrence, V. J. Cunningham, A. Dagher, T. Jones, D. J. Brooks, C. J. Bench, and P. M. Grasby. "Evidence for Striatal Dopamine Release during a Video Game." *Nature*, vol. 393, no. 6682 (May 21, 1998), 266–268.

Krug, Etienne G., Linda L. Dahlberg, James A. Mercy, Anthony B. Zwi and Rafael Lozano. *World Report on Violence and Health*. Geneva: World Health Organization, 2002.

Lincoln, Abraham. *First Inaugural Address*. New Haven, CT: Yale Law School, Avalon Project in Law History and Diplomacy, n.d.

Nealy, Elijah C. *Transgender Children and Youth: Cultivating Pride and Joy with Families in Transition*. New York: W. W. Norton & Company, 2017.

NIH. "A Family History of Alcoholism." National Institute on Alcohol Abuse and Alcoholism. https://pubs.niaaa.nih.gov/publications/familyhistory/famhist.htm. Accessed February 19, 2018.

NIH. "Genetics of Alcohol Use Disorder." www.niaaa.nih.gov/alcohol-health/overview-alcohol-consumption/alcohol-use-disorders/genetics-alcohol-use-disorders. Accessed February 21, 2018.

No Bullying. "Transgender Bullying: A National Epidemic." December 22, 2015. https://nobullying.com/transgender-bullying. Accessed March 1, 2018.

Perry, Bruce D. "Bonding and Attachment in Maltreated Children: Consequences of Emotional Neglect in Childhood." 2018. http://teacher.scholastic.com/professional/bruceperry/bonding.htm. Accessed March 30, 2018. Adapted in part from *Maltreated Children: Experience, Brain Development and the Next Generation* (New York: W. W. Norton & Company, in preparation).

Pinker, Stephen. *The Blank Slate: The Modern Denial of Human Nature*. New York: Viking, 2002.

———. *The Better Angels of Our Nature: Why Violence Has Declined*. New York: Viking, 2011.

————. *Enlightenment Now: The Case for Reason, Science, Humanism, and Progress.* New York: Viking, 2018.

Plato. *Protagoras and Meno.* Translated by Adam Beresford. London: Penguin, 2005.

Puett, Michael, and Christine Gross-Loh. *The Path: What Chinese Philosophers Can Teach Us About the Good Life.* New York: Simon & Schuster, 2016.

Redding, Carol. "The Adverse Childhood Experiences Study: Springboard to Hope." N.d. www.acestudy.org/the-ace-score.html. Accessed February 7, 2018.

Rhodes, Anne et al. "Antecedents and Sex/Gender Differences in Youth Suicidal Behaviour." *World Journal of Psychiatry*, vol. 4, no. 4 (December 14, 2014), 120–132. www.ncbi.nlm.nih.gov/pmc/articles/PMC4274584. Accessed May 18, 2018.

Rifkin, Jeremy. *The Empathic Civilization: The Race to Global Consciousness in a World of Crisis.* New York: Jeremy P. Tarcher/Penguin, 2009.

Ross, W. D. *The Right and the Good.* Edited by Phillip Stratton-Lake. Oxford: Clarendon Press, 2002.

Rutherford, Adam. "Why Racism is Not Backed by Science." *The Observer*, March 1, 2015. www.theguardian.com/science/2015/mar/01/racism-science-human-genomes-darwin. Accessed March 14, 2018.

San Francisco Zen Center. "The Ten Essential Precepts." N.d. http://sfzc.org/about-zen-center/principles-governance/ethics/ethical-principles/the-ten-essential-precepts.

Sapolsky, Robert M. *Why Zebras Don't Get Ulcers.* New York: St Martin's Griffin, 2004.

Singer, Peter. *Animal Liberation.* New York: Harper Perennial, 2009.

Smith, Adam. *The Theory of Moral Sentiments.* Mineola, NY: Dover, 2006.

————. *The Wealth of Nations.* London: Penguin, 1970.

Stevens, Jane Ellen. "Toxic Stress from Childhood Trauma Causes Obesity, Too." May 23, 2012. https://acestoohigh.com/2012/05/23/toxic-stress-from-childhood-trauma-causes-obesity-too. Accessed March 14, 2018.

Szalavitz, Maia. *Unbroken Brain: A Revolutionary New Way of Understanding Addiction.* New York: St. Martin's Press, 2016.

United Cerebral Palsy and Children's Rights. "Forgotten Children: A Case for Action for Children and Youth with Disabilities in Foster Care." A Project of United Cerebral Palsy and Children's Rights, 2006. www.childrensrights.org/wp-content/uploads/2008/06/forgotten_children_children_with_disabilities_in_foster_care_2006.pdf. Accessed April 30, 2018.

United Nations Children's Fund. *Hidden in Plain Sight: A Statistical Analysis of Violence Against Children.* New York: UNICEF, 2014.

U.S. Department of Justice, Federal Bureau of Investigation, Criminal Justice Information Services Division. "2016 Hate Crime Statistics." https://ucr.fbi.gov/hate-crime/2016/tables/table-2. Accessed March 14, 2018.

Van der Kolk, Bessel. *The Body Keeps the Score: Brain, Mind, and Body in the Healing of Trauma.* New York: Penguin, 2014.

Voelker, Dana K., Justine J. Reed and Christy Greenleaf. "Weight Status and Body Image in Adolescents: Current Perspectives." National Centre for Biotechnology Information. August 25, 2015. www.ncbi.nlm.nih.gov/pmc/articles/PMC4554432. Accessed March 14, 2018.

White, Matthew. *Atrocities: The 100 Deadliest Episodes in Human History*. New York: W. W. Norton, 2012.

Williams Institute. "New Estimates Show that 150,000 Youth Ages 13 to 17 Identify as Transgender." UCLA School of Law. January 17, 2017. https://williams institute.law.ucla.edu/research/transgender-issues/new-estimates-show-that-150000-youth-ages-13-to-17-identify-as-transgender-in-the-us. Accessed March 1, 2018.

World Bank. "Fertility Rate, Total (Births Per Woman)." Washington DC: World Bank Group. https://data.worldbank.org/indicator/SP.DYN.TFRT.IN.

Index

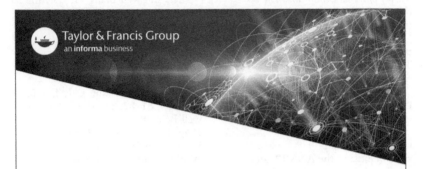

This gem of a book is an insightful guide for all caregivers who want to be a positive influence in the lives of children. The authors share touching stories and practical advice from their lives as foster parents. Their enlightened approach is a beautiful testament of the power of positive parenting.

—**Tina McMechen**, Acting Director, and Genevieve Rivera, Managing Director, American Society for the Positive Care of Children

Rather than simply being a list of "shoulds" and "shouldn'ts," this book provides perspectives on the topic of "re-parenting" children who have experienced significant trauma and chaos. This book is not just an academic treatise: its strength lies with its real-world view of working with these kids. Readers will walk away with a different perspective of the children they care for, and of themselves as caregivers. They will gain useful ideas for dealing with difficult situations, and they will gain an understanding that even when you do *everything* right, things may not always work out the way they would like. Knowing that might just help the exhausted, frustrated foster parent to provide the most nurturing environment possible.

—**Raymond D. Collings**, Associate Professor, Psychology, State University of New York, Cortland

Nurturing Strangers focuses on loving nonviolent re-parenting of children in foster care. This book is a jargon-free mix of narrative and real-life case studies, and the theory and practice of nonviolence. *Nurturing Strangers* and the authors' previous book, *Welcoming Strangers*, are the first books to apply philosophies of nonviolence directly to the care of children in the foster care system. One of the many strengths of these books are that they are not merely theoretical, but rooted in the practice of nonviolence incorporated into work with children for over thirty years. *Nurturing Strangers* is for foster carers, caseworkers, case managers, social work students, and parents, as well as the general reader interested in children who have been victims of violence in and out of the foster care system.

Andrew Fitz-Gibbon, a Fellow of the Royal Society of Arts, is Professor of Philosophy, Chair of the Philosophy Department, and Director of the Center for Ethics, Peace, and Social Justice, at the State University of New York College at Cortland. He is author or editor of thirteen books.

Jane Hall Fitz-Gibbon works in crisis support with TST BOCES, and is in Department of Social Services, co-leading courses on foster care, adoption abuse. Her latest book, *Corporal Punishment, Religion and United States Pub* published by Palgrave Macmillan in 2017.

CHILDREN / FOSTER CARE

Cover image: © Shutterstock

Routledge
Taylor & Francis Group
www.routledge.com

ISBN 978-1-138-50317-5

9 781138 503175

an **informa** business

The Sidekick

by Eve Beck
illustrated by Robbie Short

Vocabulary

construct

sidekick

unique

Word count: 1,309

Note: The total word count includes words in the running text and headings only. Numerals and words in chapter titles, captions, labels, diagrams, charts, graphs, sidebars, and extra features are not included.